Another great gift to the Church from Anderson and Mylander!
As a pastor, I know up close and personal that the great need of
today is reconciled relationships flowing from healed hearts. It's
God's work, and it's explained so clearly in this great book.

DR. STEVE GOOLD
SENIOR PASTOR, CRYSTAL EVANGELICAL FREE CHURCH
MINNEAPOLIS, MINNESOTA

As the Mideast crisis continues to intensify and every news
program is focused on discovering peace, this thoughtful book
on being a peacemaker is must reading! Anyone in the midst
of unresolved issues will discover great, usable processes
available to them in this volume.

DR. CORNELL (CORKIE) HAAN
NATIONAL FACILITATOR OF MINISTRY NETWORKS,
THE MISSION AMERICA COALITION
COFOUNDER, THE PRESIDENTIAL PRAYER TEAM

Blessed Are the Peacemakers is an essential book for anyone
interested in resolving conflicts and pursuing reconciliation in
a God-honoring and biblical way. This is an extremely practical
guide full of wisdom, understanding and examples that
virtually walk you through the process!

BILL MCCARTNEY
FOUNDER & PRESIDENT, PROMISE KEEPERS
DENVER, COLORADO

BLESSED
are the
PEACE
MAKERS

NEIL T. ANDERSON
CHARLES MYLANDER

Regal

From Gospel Light
Ventura, California, U.S.A.

Published by Regal Books
From Gospel Light
Ventura, California, U.S.A.
Printed in the U.S.A.

Regal Books is a ministry of Gospel Light, an evangelical Christian publisher
dedicated to serving the local church. We believe God's vision for Gospel Light
is to provide church leaders with biblical, user-friendly materials that will help
them evangelize, disciple and minister to children, youth and families.

It is our prayer that this Regal book will help you discover biblical truth for your
own life and help you meet the needs of others. May God richly bless you.

*For a free catalog of resources from Regal Books/Gospel Light, please call your Christian supplier
or contact us at 1-800-4-GOSPEL or www.regalbooks.com.*

ISBN 0-7394-3293-1   son and Charles Mylander

Cover and interior design by Robert Williams
Edited by Benjamin Unseth

ISBN 0-8307-2891-0

Rights for publishing this book in other languages are contracted by Gospel Light Worldwide, the international nonprofit ministry of Gospel Light. Gospel Light Worldwide
also provides publishing and technical assistance to international publishers dedicated
to producing Sunday School and Vacation Bible School curricula and books in the
languages of the world. For additional information, visit www.gospellightworldwide.org;
write to Gospel Light Worldwide, P.O. Box 3875, Ventura, CA 93006; or send an e-mail
to info@gospellightworldwide.org.

DEDICATION

Verl Lindley founded Granada Heights Friends Church and functioned as the senior pastor for 38 years. Nobody has ever read a book by Verl Lindley, because he never wrote one. People didn't scurry after every service to get a tape of his messages. And although nobody referred to Granada Heights Friends Church as Verl Lindley's church, it was there that this gentle shepherd quietly carried on a ministry of reconciliation.

He had no extraordinary gifts or talents that would put him on a national stage, although he was invited to speak nationally and internationally. We can point out other great preachers, evangelists, administrators and teachers, but we can't point out a greater pastor. Missionaries loved this church, because of the vision and care given to those called to cross-cultural service. Verl's church grew because he loved the Lord and he loved His people. Granada Heights Friends Church was built on the character of its pastor, as should be the case for every church.

His wife's service to the church was equally effective. Lois Lindley started WOW, which stands for "Women of the Word." Her message and method are still being used today by many churches. The Lindleys' four daughters are active in Christian work.

Verl and Lois's example helped to shape our own lives and also contributed greatly to this book. It has been our privilege to know and work with these servants of God. With a great deal of love and respect, we dedicate *Blessed Are the Peacemakers* to Verl and Lois Lindley. They are the epitome of what it means to be peacemakers.

Neil and Chuck

CONTENTS

FREEDOM AND HEALING

In 1980, Christine Tolbert witnessed the brutal assassination of her father, the president of Liberia. President Tolbert and 16 members of his cabinet were tied up and machine-gunned to death by a group of drunken soldiers. The president's wife and family were put under house arrest, but they eventually fled to Abidjan, Ivory Coast. For the next 15 years Liberia struggled with tribal wars.

When Christine married Lawrence Norman, they began attending a Bible study led by Ron and Doris Weeks, two veteran Navigators missionaries. It was in this Bible study that the Normans were introduced to the material of Freedom in Christ Ministries. Christine, still in agony over her brutal past, struggled with how to forgive those who had killed her father and how to bring the ministry of reconciliation to the citizens of war-torn Liberia. At the same time, the political and military leaders of her country had come to the conclusion that they could not solve their problems politically or militarily. Somehow, they reasoned, the Church needed to be involved.

Christine, who had now found the peace she was looking for through personal repentance and forgiving her father's murderers, became convinced that Freedom in Christ Ministries (FICM) was a ministry that could help her country during this window of opportunity.

The Power of Reconciliation

It was the summer of 1995 when the office of FICM received an urgent call from Ron and Doris Weeks. They asked if Neil could come to Liberia and facilitate some meetings with the leadership of this once-proud nation. Although Neil was more than willing to go, he knew that he wasn't the one who should respond to this call. His international director at that time was Joe Wasmond.[1] Joe and his wife, Kathy, had been missionaries in Africa, and they knew the African culture, as well as the message and methods of FICM.

Abandoning personal plans for summer vacation, Joe and Kathy scrambled to update Kathy's passport, obtain visas and arrange flights on Air Afrique. Upon arrival in Abidjan, they were greeted by the Normans and by 15 other Christian leaders with whom they would be living and working for the next week. The following morning they left for Monrovia, in Liberia.

The city of Monrovia had swelled from 500,000 to 2 million people due to the flood of refugees seeking asylum, who were now being fed by United Nations relief organizations. On the way to Hotel Africa, their destination, Joe and Kathy were stopped every half mile at checkpoints manned by the West African peacekeeping force, the Economic Community of West African States' Monitoring Observer Group (ECOMOG). The hotel had originally been built to facilitate an annual meeting of the presidents of the 50 African countries. But the coup in 1980, which took the life of Christine Tolbert's father, prevented the facility from ever being used for its original purpose, and it had never been maintained. It was in such horrible disrepair that it would have to be experienced to appreciate how bad it was.

The ECOMOG soldiers searched Joe and Kathy's luggage, because the hotel had been taken over by five warring factions who now occupied five of the six floors. By now the group of Christian leaders had swelled to 25, as they settled in for communal living on the remaining fourth floor. The rainy season ensured them plenty of fresh water that, unfortunately, came directly into their room through the walls and ceiling. Most of the carpet had molded away; but what remained had a pungent scent unique to Africa. Joe and Kathy were not pleased to discover that rats already occupied their twin beds.

The first two days were spent preparing the Christian leaders who had come with them to assist in the reconciliation process and to equip them for necessary follow-up. On Saturday morning, August 19, 1995, over 100 dignitaries arrived, including the media, education officials, politicians and various community groups. After an opening message, Joe Wasmond led the group through a process of personal repentance. Because reconciliation is impossible without repentance, they had to come to terms with their own sin first. In order to effect any lasting cultural change, the process had to begin with those who provided the leadership. The Holy Spirit did bring conviction that day, and each person came to terms with either his or her personal compliance or complacent attitude toward the atrocities taking place in the African countries.

This remarkable event sowed a seed that continues to germinate to this day. Christine Tolbert Norman continues to be a catalyst for forgiveness, repentance and reconciliation. She is qualified for this ministry because she has personally identified herself with the crucifixion and resurrection of our Lord and Savior Jesus Christ. As we shall explore in depth later, establishing our identity and our position in Christ is the basis for any ministry of reconciliation.

RECONCILIATION ON A PERSONAL LEVEL

In a completely different setting, the supernatural power of reconciliation was no less spectacular when a couple approached

Neil and his wife, Joanne, as they were having lunch in Yosemite National Park. When the couple introduced themselves, Neil asked, "Do I know you?"

"Well, we're a chapter in your book *Released from Bondage*,"[2] they responded. They proceeded to say they were doing well and had even taught a class on marriage in their church.

Neil's first meeting with this couple had occurred four years earlier at one of his Living Free in Christ conferences. The husband painfully spoke of how he had molested his daughter and then was forced out of his own house at gunpoint—by his own son.

The man's wife explained why she was living alone in an apartment and why the two children had left the state. Her husband had been using FICM material to seek personal help. We all have the right to throw ourselves at the throne of God and beg His mercy, and this man was no exception. He was just another example of the abused becoming an abuser.

The wife of this sexual abuser said, "I can see that he has changed, but what do I do? If I move back in with him, as he wants me to do, the children will think I am siding with him." Neil encouraged them both to attend the conference for one reason only—to get radically right with God. If they were fully reconciled to God, then maybe they could be reconciled to each other.

Now, four years after that initial meeting, this husband and wife were not only reconciled to God but also to each other. When Neil found the appropriate time and opportunity to ask how the children were doing, the couple said, "We are all reconciled to God and to each other, and our son is planning to go into full-time Christian ministry."

None of this could have happened without forgiveness, genuine repentance and faith in God.

BEYOND CONFLICT MANAGEMENT

The ministry of reconciliation is unique to the Church, and it begins with God. The apostle Paul wrote, "Now all these things are from God, who reconciled us to Himself through Christ, and gave us the ministry of reconciliation, namely, that God was in Christ reconciling the world to Himself" (2 Cor. 5:18-19, *NASB*). We must be reconciled to God before we can be reconciled to others, because the ministry of reconciliation is a supernatural ministry. That is what sets the ministry of reconciliation apart from conflict management and other secular attempts of conciliation. The latter may be helpful for coexistence, and they may even set the stage for further ministry; but they fall far short of true reconciliation.

Reconciliation is an intensely personal ministry between God and people. It may include only two individuals, or it may involve groups of people, but *it must be appropriated on a personal level*. No society can overcome racism, sexism, classism or any kind of elitism unless reconciliation has been appropriated on a personal level through genuine repentance, forgiveness and faith in God. That is why you cannot legislate reconciliation; and that is why the state or any other governing authority, other than the Church, has not been given the ministry of reconciliation. Nonspiritual authorities can negotiate a truce, but compliance will only be external and can only be maintained through the rule of law. Reconciliation, on the other hand, is a ministry of grace.

Repentance

Abusers cannot initiate the ministry of reconciliation without repentance. Social elitists cannot seek reconciliation with those who suffered at the hands of society without working to change the social structures that erected the barriers in the first place. Apart from the gospel, there is no way to substantially change the nature of fallen humanity. To ask a minority group to forgive without fully acknowledging the atrocities of the past and without working to overcome present social injustices is an affront to the victims' personal integrity.

Reparation
Likewise, for the abuser to ask forgiveness of the abused without setting the public record straight and without making reparation for the damage that was done is only an attempt to save face and do damage control. When a person has been wronged, the wrong must be made right in order for reconciliation to occur.

Forgiveness
The abused can initiate the process but cannot complete it without extending forgiveness to those who have inflicted the wound. Their own bitterness stands as a barrier between themselves and God and prevents the ministry of reconciliation from going any further. Corrie ten Boom gave us a powerful example of how the abused can take on the ministry of reconciliation. Imprisoned by the Nazi regime, she was abused and ridiculed for her beliefs. After the war, she traveled throughout Europe preaching forgiveness. One particular Sunday in Munich, Germany, a man approached her after the service to thank her for her message. Lewis Smedes wrote about what happened:

> Outside, after the service was over, a major drama of the human spirit unfolded. A man walked over to her; he reached out his hand to her, expecting her to take it. "Ja, Fraulein ten Boom, I am so glad that Jesus forgives us all our sin, just as you say."
>
> Corrie knew him. She remembered how she was forced to take showers, with other women prisoners, while this beast looked on, a leering, mocking "superman,"

guarding helpless naked women. Corrie remembered. He put his hand close to her. Her own hand froze at her side.

She could not forgive. She was stunned and terrified by her own weakness. What could she do, she who had been so sure that she had overcome the deep hurt and the desperate hate and had arrived at forgiving, what could she do now that she was confronted by a man she could not forgive?

She prayed, "Jesus, I can't forgive this man. Forgive me." At once, in some wonderful way that she was not prepared for, she felt forgiven. Forgiven for not forgiving.

At that moment—in the power of the fundamental feeling—her hand went up, took the hand of her enemy, and released him. In her heart she freed him from her terrible past. And she freed herself from hers. [3]

Corrie ten Boom, Christine Tolbert Norman and many other saints are examples of what the ministry of reconciliation is all about. The day they identified with the sufferings of Christ, they were set free from their past and made new creations in Christ. That's what we're going to talk about in this book. We will roughly follow the order of 2 Corinthians 5:14-21. This passage identifies every born-again person with Christ and presents each one as a new creation in Christ (see vv. 14-17). As children of God we have been given the ministry of reconciliation (vv. 18-19), of which we are to be good ambassadors (vv. 20-21).

FIRST THE SOLUTION AND THEN THE APPLICATION

In the first half of the book we will explore in depth the theological basis of reconciliation—what it is and how Jesus brings about this supernatural transaction. We will look at the example and ministry of Christ. Then we will discover what it means to be a new creation in Christ. We have to identify with the death, burial and resurrection of Christ if we are going to be the people God has created us to be. We cannot impart to others what we do not possess ourselves. Every Christian ministry begins with our righteous relationship with God. Once we have been reconciled to Him, then we can be reconciled to others. And only when that is accomplished can we properly exercise the ministry of reconciliation.

In the second half of the book, we will seek to understand the ministry of reconciliation through practical application. First we will explore the dynamics of conflict management and contrast that with the more comprehensive ministry of reconciliation. We will explain repentance and when it is appropriate to make reparation. It is not uncommon for some to seek reconciliation without repentance; but that is impossible. We will also explain what it means to forgive from the heart and how to seek the forgiveness of others.

Finding our identity and freedom in Christ is always possible, because it only depends on our relationship with God. God's unconditional love and forgiveness have made it possible for all to be reconciled to Him. However, being reconciled to another person may not always be possible when that person is unwilling. We will share a process for bringing about reconciliation when two people or people groups desire to be reconciled.

We will share how a perpetrator who comes under conviction can be reconciled with the victim. We will also share how the victim who has forgiven the abuser and found freedom in Christ can have a ministry of reconciliation.

Church discipline is also a ministry of reconciliation. We will discuss a process that can lead to repentance as a ministry of mercy and grace. The goal is to help people realize what their unforgiving attitudes and actions are doing to them and to others, so they will repent. If they refuse to repent, then they must face the consequences of losing the privilege of fellowship with the Church.

Finally, we will discuss what it means to be a good ambassador for Christ. Too often the Church has been part of the problem instead of the answer. We cannot carry out a ministry of reconciliation if we have been guilty of racism, sexism or other forms of elitism. Too often we have been guilty of exclusion when we should have been setting the example of inclusion. Abusive leadership, sectarianism, liberalism and legalism have kept the Church from exercising the ministry of reconciliation.

To ensure that you are a part of the answer and not a part of the problem, we encourage you to examine your own heart and prayerfully consider the words of Paul in Colossians 3:9-11 (*NASB*):

> Do not lie to one another, since you laid aside the old self with its evil practices, and have put on the new self who is being renewed to a true knowledge according to the image of the One who created him—a renewal in which there is no distinction between Greek and Jew, circumcised and uncircumcised, barbarian, Scythian, slave and freeman, but Christ is all, and in all.

It has been our privilege to help victims throughout the world to resolve their personal and spiritual conflicts and to find freedom in Christ. Now we would like to take the next step and explain the God-ordained ministry of reconciliation. It is our prayer that you will become better equipped to be a minister of reconciliation and to be a good ambassador for Christ.

Neil Anderson and Chuck Mylander

HOW PEACEMAKERS ARE BORN

God was reconciling the world to himself in Christ, not counting men's sins against them. And he has committed to us the message of reconciliation.

2 CORINTHIANS 5:19

PART I

CHAPTER I

JESUS THE RECONCILER

Colossians 1:19-23

God has a one-item agenda, listed in one expressive and inclusive word—reconciliation.

Samuel Hines, *Beyond Rhetoric: Reconciliation as a Way of Life*

He had planned a special meeting with this man they called Jesus. They would have an intimate lunch together in his home and discuss religion. But the Pharisee's plans were dashed when a woman, simply known as a "sinner," crashed the party. "She brought an alabaster vial of perfume, and standing behind [Jesus] at His feet, weeping, she began to wet His feet with her tears, and kept wiping them with the hair of her head, and kissing His feet, and anointing them with the perfume" (Luke 7:37-38, *NASB*). This was unacceptable to this pious Jew, who thought to himself, "If this man were a prophet He would know who and what sort of person this woman is who is touching Him, that she is a sinner" (v. 39, *NASB*).

Jesus did know what sort of woman she was, and He also knew what this Pharisee was thinking, supposedly to himself. Jesus said, "Simon, I have something to say to you." And Simon replied, "Say it, Teacher" (v. 40, *NASB*). What follows in Luke's narrative is another embarrassing moment for those who do not know the real Jesus or His message of forgiveness and reconciliation. Jesus would have dined with either the Pharisee or the "sinner," but He chose this grateful woman who showed more love, because she was more aware of her need to be forgiven. We all stand on equal ground when it comes to our need to be forgiven by God.

THE ALL-INCLUSIVE JESUS

Mary was a virgin when she found herself with child by the power of the Holy Spirit (see Matt. 1:18). Unlike the rest of the fallen citizens of this world, Jesus was born both physically and spiritually alive. He was fully God and fully human. Tracing the bloodline of Jesus back to Abraham, Matthew reveals Jesus as the messianic King, who sits on the throne of David. Jesus shared the same physical heritage of all Semitic people, including Arabs and Jews. Luke goes even further when he traces the lineage of Jesus all the way back to Adam and declares Jesus to be "the son of Adam, the son of God" (Luke 3:38, *NASB*).

We are all descendants of Adam and Eve (the mother of all), and we all share a common humanity. No race is superior to another, and we all stand in need of redemption. Our current social standing carries no weight in heaven. When Jesus became our Kinsman-Redeemer, as powerfully illustrated in the book of Ruth (see 3:9,12; 4:1,3,6,8,14), it was for all the people of the world, because Jesus was everyone's physical kin. This all-inclusive message is reflected in the nature of God. "For God so loved the *world*, that He gave His only begotten Son, that *whoever* believes in Him should not perish, but have eternal life" (John 3:16, *NASB*, emphasis added).

Jesus spent most of His life in Palestine, the crossroads between the East and the West. Palestine would be considered by many to be more Asian and African, even though it was ruled by European Rome. Most of His ministry was in Galilee, away from the Temple in Jerusalem, the center of Judaism. The Jews made up less than a third of the population in Galilee, which was the home of Assyrians, Syrians, Babylonians, Persians, Macedonians, Egyptians and Romans. We invite you to take another look at this Man for all seasons and for all people.

When traveling to Jerusalem, Jesus did not seek a route *around* Samaria, as other Jews did. He traveled through Samaria and interacted with these "half-breed" descendants of the rebellious northern tribes of Israel. Coming to one city, Jesus asked a Samaritan woman to give him a drink from Jacob's well. The Samaritan woman said to Him, " 'How is it that You, being a Jew, ask me for a drink since I am a Samaritan woman?' (For Jews have no dealings with Samaritans)" (John 4:9, *NASB*). Jews may not have had dealings with Samaritans, but Jesus did. He deals with all the citizens of this earth.

Jesus rebuked a self-righteous Jewish lawyer by telling the story of the Samaritan, who proved to be a good neighbor by tending to the needs of a victimized man, while a priest and Levite ignored him (see Luke 10:30-37). When the moral standards of God make us uncomfortable, the temptation is to redefine terminology in order to accommodate our sinful attitudes and actions. Consequently, our "neighbors" become only those who fit into our racial and cultural comfort zones. But Jesus would not let the lawyer off the hook, and neither will He let us justify our prejudices. The neighbors we are called to love include all the marginalized people of this world.

DEFINING RECONCILIATION

Most evangelical Christians acknowledge that we have all sinned and fallen short of the glory of God (see Rom. 3:23), and anyone who calls upon the name of the Lord will be saved (see Rom.

10:13). No committed Christian would deny anyone access to God through Christ—there is general agreement that the gospel is to be taken to the ends of the earth. Yet Christians do not always apply the universal gospel and its promise of reconciliation to their own relationships. The Jews understood reconciliation to be an issue between themselves and God, while the Greeks understood it to be an issue between themselves and others. They were both right, but we cannot participate in any ministry of reconciliation until we are first reconciled to God. Establishing peace with God first is essential if we want peace in our relationships.

Several years ago, a ministry couple was referred to me (Neil) for counseling. If they did not get some help soon, they were going to be dismissed from their church. They came through the door in a combative mood. I refereed the fight for a few minutes and sensed that their situation was hopeless unless I could get them on another track. I said, "I think you should forget about your marriage. You are so torn up on the inside that I doubt if you could get along with your dog right now." It was obvious they were not right with God; how could they be right with each other? I asked the wife if it were possible for her to get away for a few days or even a couple of weeks. She said she could and was even willing to do so. Her family had a cabin in the nearby mountains.

I gave her a set of tapes on resolving personal and spiritual conflicts. I encouraged her to listen to them and apply them to her life. I even suggested that she not do it for the purpose of saving her marriage but for the sake of her own personal relationship with God. I asked her husband to do the same while she was away. They both agreed. I did not see either of them for three years. One Sunday, after church, we met again by chance in a restaurant. They were happy to report that they were doing much better.

I have seen this kind of transformation take place a number of times at our conferences. Couples come as a last resort and leave hand in hand, yet we hardly even talked about marriage. Only after getting right with God can we be the friends, spouses and parents God wants us to be.

The Law could not reconcile humanity to God, and that is probably why there is no Hebrew equivalent for the Greek word *katallage* (reconciliation), which is found four times in the New Testament. Three times it is used to refer to the reconciliation between God and humankind (see Rom. 5:11; 2 Cor. 5:18-19). The fourth occurrence is found in Romans 11:15, in which Paul speaks of the offer of reconciliation that has been extended to the whole Gentile world, as well as to his Jewish brothers and sisters, even though the nation of Israel had rejected Jesus as the Messiah. In addition, there are three intensive forms of reconciliation used in Ephesians 2:16 and Colossians 1:20-21, which could be translated "to reconcile fully."

No Longer Alienated from God

The doctrine of reconciliation brings into focus the alienation from God that we all experienced—and perhaps still do. It has to do with the removal of that which stands in the way of our relationship with Him. Sin separated us from God. In order to be reconciled with Him, the sin issue had to be dealt with. We were incapable of not sinning, and there was nothing we could do to atone for our own sins. In other words, we could not initiate reconciliation with God. He had to take the initiative, and He did. "For it was the Father's good pleasure for all the fulness to dwell in Him, and through Him to reconcile *all things* to Himself, having made peace through the blood of His cross" (Col. 1:19-20, *NASB*, emphasis added).

Reconciliation is costly. Our heavenly Father had to sacrifice His only Son in order for our sins to be forgiven. Jesus suffered the agony of taking upon Himself all the sins of the world. "For the death that He died, He died to sin, once for all" (Rom. 6:10, *NASB*). "God was in Christ reconciling the world to Himself, not counting their trespasses against them, and He has committed to us the word of reconciliation" (2 Cor. 5:19, *NASB*). His sacrifice is our salvation.

No Longer at Home in the World

Proclaiming the word of reconciliation can also be costly. If you are not willing to sacrifice something of your time or self, then do not consider the ministry of reconciliation.

Sin has not only separated people from God but from each other as well. Every successful missionary has had to sacrifice something to bring the gospel message to others—money, career plans, prestige, comfort, home, family and friends. Even sharing your faith at home requires a sacrifice of time; and the risk of rejection may have social consequences. Witnessing is not popular in any culture where the discussion of politics and religion has a tendency to polarize people. Mediating a dispute between two people is tiring work, but you are doing the work of Christ, and there are great rewards.

> **SIN HAS NOT ONLY SEPARATED PEOPLE FROM GOD BUT FROM EACH OTHER AS WELL.**

Although there is a price to pay, nobody had to pay the price that Jesus did; but He did it with joy, and so can we. Therefore, "Let us run with endurance the race that is set before us, fixing our eyes on Jesus, the author and perfecter of faith, who for the joy set before Him endured the cross, despising the shame, and has sat down at the right hand of the throne of God" (Heb. 12:1-2, *NASB*).

Neil was doing some one-on-one personal evangelism at Long Beach State University, using a small survey as his entrée for sharing the gospel. When he asked a Native American who Jesus Christ was, the man responded, "A figment of your imagination."

Neil continued, "According to your understanding, how does one become a Christian?"

"Applied stupidity," the man answered. Not exactly ripe fruit!

Rather than press the matter, Neil asked, "Apparently something has turned you off to Christianity. Would you care to share your experience?"

For the next 30 minutes, this victim of racial discrimination shared his observations and experiences. Neil responded by saying, "Thank you for sharing that. It helps me to understand you by knowing what you have gone through. If I had the same experience, I would probably feel the same way. If someone should ever ask you what true Christianity is, maybe you could give him this." Neil handed him a gospel tract. The man took it and left. That small sacrifice of time and risk of rejection resulted in pure joy because of the opportunity to direct someone to the true gospel message.

More Than Forgiven

Reconciliation parallels the idea of and is similar to the doctrine of justification (see Rom. 5:9-10). That is because the means of reconciliation is the death of God's Son (see Rom. 5:10), as it is also the means for justification. The purpose of the sacrificial death was to atone for our sins, and the imputation of His righteousness to us (regeneration) is the grounds for removing the cause of our alienation from God. He will no longer count our trespasses against us. Under the New Covenant, He will remember our sins no more (see Heb. 10:17).

God has forgiven every born-again child of God. Forgiveness means that He will not take into account our past offenses and use them against us in the final judgment. "As far as the east is from the west, so far has He removed our transgressions from us" (Ps. 103:12, *NASB*).

Reconciliation is more than justification, however. Reconciliation is the *restoration* of a relationship between two parties. For instance, Paul gives instruction for the reconciliation between a husband and wife (see 1 Cor. 7:11). Reconciliation is the process of overcoming the enmity that has disrupted a relationship. In Paul's writings, reconciliation is contrasted with enmity, alienation and hostility (see Rom. 5:10; Eph. 2:14-22; Col. 1:21). In the positive sense, it has the outcome of peace. Overcoming the reason for the alienation brings about a condition of peaceful coexistence. "Peace" is an inclusive term referring to the restoration of the relationship between God and humanity. "Therefore having been justified by faith, we have peace with God through our Lord Jesus Christ" (Rom. 5:1, *NASB*).

RESPONDING PROPERLY TO THE GOSPEL

Jesus took the initiative and did all that was necessary for us to be reconciled to Him. It can be argued that God forgives us all, since Jesus died once for all. But not all have been reconciled to Him. That is why He "gave us the ministry of reconciliation" (2 Cor. 5:18, *NASB*). "Therefore, we are ambassadors for Christ, as though God were entreating through us; we beg you on behalf of Christ, be reconciled to God" (v. 20, *NASB*).

In the same way, we can forgive those who have offended us; but that does not mean we are reconciled to them. Paul wrote, "If possible, so far as it depends on you, be at peace with all men" (Rom. 12:18, *NASB*). But it does not fully depend on us, and therefore it is not always possible. If the offending party does not want to be reconciled, then it is not possible. To complete the process of reconciliation, the offending party has to assume personal responsibility.

> OUR CAPACITY TO LOVE ONE ANOTHER COMES FROM THE PRESENCE OF GOD WITHIN US. ALL THE INSTRUCTIONS FOR RIGHTEOUS LIVING WITH OTHERS FLOW OUT OF OUR RELATIONSHIP WITH GOD.

The important point that we want to stress here is this: Reconciliation in any relationship requires the cooperation of both parties, and there cannot be complete reconciliation between two mortals unless we are fully reconciled to God. Reconciliation is supernatural work. Our capacity to love one another comes from the presence of God within us. All the instructions for righteous living with others flow out of our relationship with God. "We love, because He first loved us" (1 John 4:19, *NASB*). "Be merciful, just as your Father is merciful" (Luke 6:36, *NASB*). "Be kind to one another, tenderhearted, forgiving each other, just as God in Christ also has forgiven you" (Eph. 4:32, *NASB*). As God has been gracious to us, we are to be gracious to others.

What must we do then to be reconciled to God? Paul continues in Colossians 1:21-23:

And although you were formerly alienated and hostile in mind, engaged in evil deeds, yet He has now reconciled you in His fleshly body through death, in order to present you before Him holy and blameless and beyond reproach—if indeed you continue in the faith firmly established and steadfast, and not moved away from the hope of the gospel that you have heard, which was proclaimed in all creation under heaven, and of which I, Paul, was made a minister.

Paul has clearly established that faith and faith alone is the basis for our salvation. "For by grace you have been saved through faith; and that not of yourselves, it is the gift of God; not as a result of works, that no one should boast" (Eph. 2:8-9, *NASB*). The ultimate purpose according to the above passage is to present us holy and blameless before our heavenly Father. That is going to require us to change; and that means repentance.

The continuation of Paul's thinking in Ephesians reads, "For we are His workmanship, created in Christ Jesus for good works, which God prepared beforehand, that we should walk in them" (Eph. 2:10, *NASB*). The same sequence is found in Titus: "He saved us, not on the basis of deeds which we have done in righteousness, but according to His mercy, by the washing of regeneration and renewing by the Holy Spirit . . . so that those who have believed God may be careful to engage in good deeds" (3:5,8, *NASB*).

A changed life is the proof of our repentance. John the Baptist rebuked the Pharisees and Sadducees who requested baptism. He called them snakes, who should "bring forth fruit in keeping with repentance" (Matt. 3:8, *NASB*). Paul preached to everyone "that they should repent and turn to God, performing deeds appropriate to repentance" (Acts 26:20, *NASB*). James shows the connection between faith and works when he wrote, "But someone may well say, 'You have faith and I have works; show me your faith without the works, and I will show you my faith by my works'" (2:18, *NASB*). James is saying that biblical faith, will affect how we live, and if it does not, then we really do not believe. People do not always live what they profess, but they always live what they believe.

Therefore, to be reconciled to God, we must believe that He has died for our sins and given us a new life in Christ. Jesus has accomplished for us what we could not do for ourselves. That is why we must fully trust in the finished work of Christ and believe that we are what we are by the grace of God. By His death we are forgiven, and by His resurrection we have new life in Christ. If our faith is legitimate, it will result in a changed life that is set on the course of conforming to the image of God.

> # THE NEW LIFE WE HAVE IN CHRIST IS WHAT EMPOWERS US TO CHANGE.

The new life we have in Christ is what empowers us to change. Jesus makes this point very clear when He says, "You will know them by their fruits" (Matt. 7:20, *NASB*), "By this all men will know that you are My disciples, if you have love for one another" (John 13:35, *NASB*), and "My Father [is] glorified [by this], that you bear much fruit, and so prove to be My disciples" (John 15:8, *NASB*).

To better understand reconciliation, consider the difference between a relationship and peaceful harmony between two parties. What determines whether you are related to one another is different from that which determines how well you live in harmony with one another.

When I was physically born, I was a child of Marvin Anderson. Was there anything I could do after my physical birth that would change the fact that we had a father-son relationship? What if I disobeyed him or ran away? He would still be my father, because we were blood related. It is a biological fact. However, there was something I could do or not do that would cause me to no longer live in harmony with my earthly father, and I learned almost every way by the time I was five years old. Like Jesus, the only perfect example, I learned obedience from the things which I suffered (see Heb. 5:8). But it was not a question of my relatedness. That had already been established. If I trusted my father and obeyed him, we lived in harmony with one another and there was peace between us.

Years later I received Christ and trusted in His works and His righteousness to save me. I was born again. Concerning this new birth, John wrote, "But as many as received Him, to them He gave the right to become children of God, even to those who believe in His name, who were born not of blood nor of the will of the flesh nor of the will of man, but of God" (John 1:12-13, *NASB*). I was not saved by how I behaved. I was saved by how I believed. I did not save myself. Jesus saved me. I did not earn it; it was a free gift of God. I did not deserve it. I became a child of God by the grace of God. Being a child of God, is there something I can or cannot do that will change the fact that God is my heavenly Father? No, because we are blood related! (I realize the theological differences that exist among believers concerning the perseverance of the saints; but that is not the point I am trying to make.)

Whether I have a relationship with God and whether I am living in harmony with Him are two different issues. If we had to first become perfect before we could have a relationship with God, then we would all be doomed. If we had to stay perfect in order to remain His children, we would likewise be doomed. Whether we live in harmony with God as His children is no longer an issue of the blood shed by our Lord Jesus Christ; it is related to our willingness to trust and obey Him. If we trust God and obey His commands, then we will live in harmony with Him. If we do not perfectly believe or obey Him, we do not lose our salvation, but we also do not walk in the full victory God intended for us. Living in harmony with God is living in communion with

Him and in community with our brothers and sisters in Christ.

Saved

The question that remains is: Are we fully reconciled to God at the moment of our new birth in Christ? That question's answer is similar to the answer for this question: Are we fully saved? As defined in Scripture, salvation as applied to the believer is past, present and future tense. In other words, we *have been* saved, we *are being* saved and someday we *shall be* fully saved from the wrath that is to come. Notice how Paul uses the past tense in referring to our salvation. "Join with me in suffering for the gospel, by the power of God, who has saved us and called us to a holy life—not because of anything we have done but because of his own purpose and grace" (2 Tim. 1:8-9; see also Eph. 2:4-5,8; Titus 3:4-5).

Something definitive happened the moment we were born again. We were transferred as God's possessions out of the kingdom of darkness and into the kingdom of His beloved Son (see Col. 1:13; Eph. 1:13-14) and were made new creations in Christ (see 2 Cor. 5:17). The Lord wants us to have the assurance of our salvation. According to John, "These things I have written to you who believe in the name of the Son of God, in order that you may know that you have eternal life" (1 John 5:13, *NASB*). "The Spirit Himself testifies with our spirit that we are God's children" (Rom. 8:16). But we have not yet experienced the totality of our salvation.

We are also in the process of being saved. "The message of the cross is foolishness to those who are perishing, but to us who are being saved it is the power of God" (1 Cor. 1:18; see also 2 Cor. 2:15). We do not work for our salvation; rather, we work out what God has already born in us (see Phil. 2:12).

Finally, some aspects of our salvation are yet future. "Since we have now been justified by his blood, how much more shall we be saved from God's wrath through him!" (Rom. 5:9; see also Rom. 13:11; Heb. 9:28).

Sanctified

The same is true for sanctification, which is God's will for our lives (see 1 Thess. 4:3). The doctrine of sanctification begins at our new birth and concludes with our glorification in heaven. We *have been* sanctified (see 1 Cor. 1:2; Acts 20:32), we *are being* sanctified (see Rom. 6:22; 2 Cor. 7:1), and someday we *shall be* fully sanctified (see Eph. 5:25-27; 1 Thess. 3:12-13; 5:23-24). When used in the past tense, sanctification is referred to as positional sanctification. Present tense is progressive, or experiential, sanctification. Positional sanctification is the basis for progressive sanctification. We are not trying to become children of God; we are children of God who are becoming like Christ. Progressive sanctification is making real in our experience what has already happened to us in our new birth. "At the same moment that we became justified and sanctified positionally, the Spirit of God came into our lives and began the process of transforming our character through progressive sanctification, or Christian growth."[1]

In a *judicial* sense we are fully reconciled to God. The barrier of sin has been removed, and we are no longer alienated from Him. We are His children, and we are in the process of conforming to His image. Having been justified (forgiven), we have peace with God (see Rom. 5:1). Whether or not we sense that peace depends on whether we are living in harmony with Him. We cannot continue to live in sin and sense the peace of God. We are positionally reconciled to God, and that is the basis for making it real in our experience. Positional truth is real truth, the foundation for experiencing God and growing in grace.

WHO WE ARE IN CHRIST

It has been my privilege to work with thousands of people around the world who are struggling in their faith. Most have no assurance of their salvation. The idea of being reconciled to God is in the category of wishful thinking at best and in the category of severe doubt or denial at worst. These professing Christians (or at least those who thought they were or wanted to be), who were struggling with fear, anger, depression, compulsive behaviors, addictions, bitterness, mental torment, etc., all had one thing in common. None of them knew who he or she was "in Christ" nor understood what it meant to be a child of God, and all of them were struggling with interpersonal relationships. If the Holy Spirit had been bearing witness with their spirit (see Rom 8:16), why were they not sensing it?

Over the years, Chuck and I have progressively learned how to help people resolve their personal and spiritual conflicts and find their freedom in Christ through genuine repentance. If they successfully submitted to God and resisted the devil (see Jas. 4:7), they would have a sense of inner peace and a new understanding of their adoption as children of God. Paul wrote, "Because you are sons, God sent the Spirit of his Son into our hearts, the Spirit who calls out, 'Abba, Father'" (Gal. 4:6).

An example of the above was an undergraduate student who came to see me with some questions about Satanism. I answered some of her questions and then suggested that she probably should not be doing that kind of research in her condition. When she asked why, I said, "Because you are not experiencing your freedom in Christ."

"What do you mean by that?" she asked.

I told her that she was probably having a difficult time paying attention in Bible classes, that her devotional and prayer life were probably nonexistent and that she was probably struggling with a low sense of worth and a poor identity.

She thought I was reading her mind; but I simply had enough experience working with people to be able to sense that there were many unresolved conflicts in her life. She got permission to take my graduate-level course on resolving personal and spiritual conflicts that summer in a one-week intensive program, and she wrote this letter to me:

> What I have discovered this last week is this feeling of control. Like my mind is my own. I haven't sat and had these strung-out periods of thought and contemplation, i.e., conversations with myself. My mind just simply feels quieted. It is really a strange feeling.
>
> My emotions have been stable. I haven't felt depressed once this week. My will is mine. I feel like I have been able to choose my life abiding in Christ. Scripture seems different. I have a totally different perspective. I understand what it is saying. I feel left alone but not in a bad way. I'm not lonely, just a single person. For the first time I believe I actually understand what it means to be a Christian, who Christ is and who I am in Him.
>
> I feel capable of helping people and capable of handling myself. I've been a codependent for years, but this last week I haven't had the slightest feeling or need for someone.
>
> I guess I am describing what it is like to be at peace. I feel this quiet, soft joy in my heart. I have been more friendly with strangers and comfortable. There hasn't been this struggle to get through the day, and there is the fact that I have been participating in life and not passively critically watching it. Thank you for lending me your hope. I believe I have my own now in Christ.

The woman's experience is not uncommon; in fact, the Bible's message of peace and reconciliation is reaching people all over the world. At the beginning of the last century, the Christian population in Africa was only about 5 percent. Now it is approximately 50 percent. Missionaries told Africans that they could have all their sins forgiven and have eternal life if they would just trust in Jesus, and many did. Unfortunately, when social conflicts started to arise, many African Christians fell back on their tribal identities and pagan practices. That probably would not have happened if they had repented and been fully established in Christ as children of God. There are, however, some remarkable accounts of committed Christians in Liberia and Rwanda who would not participate in tribal wars and acts of genocide.

Although it may be easier to see the problem in other countries, we too have our tribal identities and pagan practices. Peace with God is meant to permeate our interpersonal relationships. If we are going to see reconciliation between brothers and sisters in Christ and unity among believers, we must repent and discover our identity, freedom and peace in Christ. God did not have to repent in order to take the initiative for us to be reconciled to Him. He did have to find a means by which we could be forgiven, and He did. In order for us to be reconciled to Him, we must put our trust in Him. If we want to experience reconciliation with God and carry on the ministry of reconciliation, then we must repent and commit ourselves to be like Jesus, the all-inclusive One.

CHAPTER 2

RECONCILED TO GOD

Romans 5:8-11

The Ministry of Reconciliation
Originates with God, not man
Is personally experienced
Is universally inclusive
Is without condemnation
Is delivered by men
Is owned and accredited by God
Is voluntarily accepted
Achieves what otherwise is impossible
Is experienced moment by moment.
Ray Stedman, *Authentic Christianity*

The Body of Christ is a living organism whose members are empowered by God to build up one another in a loving atmosphere of mutual trust and respect. It is a redeeming community where we find wholeness and meaning in life. Every member is gifted by God and of equal worth in His sight. We are instructed to accept one another, greet one another, encourage one another and love one another. In other words, we are to extend to others what God has freely given to us. Concerning the Church, Paul wrote, "I write so that you may know how one ought to conduct himself in the household of God, which is the church of the living God, the pillar and support of the truth" (1 Tim. 3:15, *NASB*).

All this breaks down, however, when a local body of believers is headed for a church split. People are either ignorant of how they ought to conduct themselves with one another, or they simply disregard clear instructions from Scripture. Power struggles develop, people take sides, and hurtful words are said in anger. Roots of bitterness spring up and many are defiled (see Heb. 12:15). In other words, they resort to their tribal identities and pagan practices! It was from this kind of situation that a pastor wrote me (Neil) the following letter:

> I'm the founding pastor of this church having begun 16 years ago and now I find myself in the first steps of recovering from a church split. I have never known pain like this, but I am finding it a tremendous time of learning and growth in the Lord. Your book *Victory over the Darkness* has been especially helpful in that I have tried to find too much of my identity in what I do as a pastor and not enough in who I am as a saint.

This pastor discovered through pain and brokenness that his personal identity, acceptance, security and significance are found in his eternal relationship with God. It requires a degree of brokenness for us to fully identify with Christ in His death, burial and resurrection. It would be tragic to suffer through personal conflicts and never come to an understanding of the rich inheritance that we all have in Christ. Under the inspiration of God, Paul obviously knew that we would have difficulty comprehending who we are in Christ and the rich inheritance that we have in Him. So he prays for divine enlightenment: "I pray also that the eyes of your heart may be enlightened in order that you may know the hope to which he has called you, the riches of his glorious inheritance in the saints" (Eph. 1:18). Part of this ignorance comes from not understanding the full gospel as stated by Paul in Romans 5:10, "When we were God's enemies, we were reconciled to him through the death of his Son, how much more, having been reconciled, shall we be saved through his life!"

God demonstrated His love for us by sacrificing His own Son (see 1 John 3:16). If we could just convince believers that God unconditionally loved and accepted them, we would see a lot more inner peace and harmony among the members in our churches. But it is not enough to know that we are no longer destined for hell. The gospel offers us much more, since we are also saved by His life. This is even more good news: We have now received reconciliation with God.

In America, however, we are laboring under an incomplete presentation of the gospel. We have presented Jesus as the Messiah who died for our sins; and if we receive Him into our lives, we will get to go to heaven when we die. There are two problems with that presentation. First, it would give you the impression that eternal life is something we get when we die. That is not true. Eternal life is something we get the moment we receive Christ. "He who has the Son has the life; he who does not have the Son of God does not have the life" (1 John 5:12, *NASB*).

Second, it is only part of the gospel. Too often we have taken the resurrection out of our gospel presentation. Jesus went to the Cross and died for our sins. Is that the whole gospel? Absolutely not! Thank God for Good Friday, but the resurrection of Christ is what we celebrate every spring. Jesus not only came to give us heaven; He is our life *today* (see Col. 3:4).

Paul says that without the resurrection we have no hope (see 1 Cor. 15:12-19). Christians who believe only a third of the gospel see themselves as forgiven sinners instead of redeemed saints. Eternal life is not something we get when we die. If we do not have eternal life before we die physically, all we would have to look forward to is hell. Paul says that we have now (not later) received the reconciliation. As born-again believers, our souls are in union with God. We are new creations in Christ. This new spiritual life is most often portrayed in the Epistles as being "in Christ," or "in Him." For every verse that proclaims that Christ is within us, there are 10 verses explaining that we are in Christ.

> **TRYING TO DO THE WORK OF RECONCILIATION WITH ONLY THE WORDS OF CHRIST WILL NOT WORK. WE MUST HAVE THE LIFE OF CHRIST—HIS POWER WORKING THROUGH US.**

Trying to do the work of reconciliation with only the words of Christ will not work. We must have the life of Christ—His power working through us. This is where attempts at reconciliation with one another break down. First, we ourselves fail to recognize the other person or people as children of God. Consequently, we use exclusive language such as "you people" or "those people." Reconciliation is not going to take place if we perceive others as "one of them" instead of as "one of us." Second, if we have not resolved our own issues with God, our attempts to be reconciled to others or initiate a ministry of reconciliation are "in the flesh" instead of "in the Spirit." Begrudgingly trying to be obedient to the law is not going to bear fruit. Being coerced by others to obey Scripture will not work either. Reconciliation is a heart issue, and if either party's heart is not right with God, it will not take place. Such attempts will prove to be inadequate as Paul points out in 2 Corinthians 3:5, "Not that we are adequate in ourselves to consider anything as coming from ourselves, but our adequacy is from God."

Reconciliation is a New Covenant ministry. The minister of reconciliation needs a new heart and a new spirit, as Ezekiel prophesied, "I will give them an undivided heart and put a new spirit in them; I will remove from them their heart of stone and give them a heart of flesh. Then they will follow my decrees and be careful to keep my laws. They will be my people, and I will be their God" (11:19-20; see also 36:26-27).

The New Covenant prophesied by Jeremiah not only ensures our forgiveness but also the enabling presence of God within us (see Jer. 31:31-40; Heb. 8:8-12). Apart from Christ we can do nothing (see John 15:5). Reconciliation is a matter of the heart, not of external conformity to some rigid standard, no matter how noble it may seem.

Our identity comes from our new life in Christ.

> Yet to all who received him, to those who believed in his name, he gave the right to become children of God (John 1:12).

> How great is the love the Father has lavished on us, that we should be called children of God! . . . Dear friends, now we are children of God, and what we will be has not yet been made known. But we know that when he appears, we shall be like him, for we shall see him as he is. Everyone who has this hope in him purifies himself, just as he is pure (1 John 3:1-3).

Putting our hope in God and knowing who we are in Christ is the foundation for growing in grace and righteous living.

When we were dead in our trespasses and sins, we had no choice but to find our identity, purpose and meaning in life in the natural order of this fallen world. It is natural to find our identity in our physical heritage, vocation and social status. This inevitably leads to classism, elitism, sexism and racism. The gospel is all-inclusive and makes the ground level before the Cross with every believer afforded the same access. We all have front-row seats, and our Father bought the tickets. The other natural tendency is to establish our identity by the things we do. Therefore, many Christians see themselves as pastors, counselors, carpenters, migrant farmworkers, manicurists, etc. What happens then, when people lose their jobs or can no longer perform as they once could? Do they lose their identity? What we do does not determine who we are. Who we are determines what we do. So, who are we, according to Scripture?

Finding his identity in a ministerial role probably led the above pastor to shepherd God's people in a way he now regrets. Discovering his identity in Christ will affect how he lives out his calling in life, and chances are he is now experiencing a lot less conflict. That will be even more true if he teaches his congregation who they are in Christ and enables them to be all that God created them to be. Nobody can consistently behave in a way that is inconsistent with what one believes about oneself and God. Conflict resolution begins with a biblical understanding of who God is, who we are in Christ and how He meets all our needs according to His riches in glory. The critical needs and the ones most powerfully met in Christ are the "being" needs. His gave us new life and a new identity and meets our needs for acceptance, security and significance, as follows:

WHO I AM IN CHRIST

I Am Accepted in Christ

I am God's child (John 1:12).

I am Christ's friend (John 15:15).

I have been justified (Rom. 5:1).

I am united with the Lord, and I am one spirit with Him (1 Cor. 6:17).

I have been bought with a price: I belong to God (1 Cor. 6:19-20).

I am a member of Christ's Body (1 Cor. 12:27).

I am a saint, a holy one (Eph. 1:1).

I have been adopted as God's child (Eph. 1:5).

I have direct access to God through the Holy Spirit (Eph. 2:18).

I have been redeemed and forgiven of all my sins (Col. 1:14).

I am complete in Christ (Col. 2:10).

I Am Secure in Christ

I am free forever from condemnation (Rom. 8:1-2).

I am assured that all things work together for good (Rom. 8:28).

I am free from any condemning charges against me (Rom. 8:31-34).

I cannot be separated from the love of God (Rom. 8:35-39).

I have been established (made firm), anointed and sealed by God (2 Cor. 1:21-22).

I am confident that the good work God has begun in me will be perfected (Phil. 1:6).

I am a citizen of heaven (Phil. 3:20).

I am hidden with Christ in God (Col. 3:3).

I have not been given a spirit of fear, but of power, of love and of a sound mind (2 Tim. 1:7).

I can find grace and mercy to help in time of need (Heb. 4:16).

I am born of God, and the evil one cannot touch me (1 John 5:18).

I Am Significant in Christ

I am the salt of the earth and the light of the world (Matt. 5:13-14).

I am a branch of the true vine, Jesus, a channel of His life (John 15:1,5).

I have been chosen and appointed by God to bear fruit (John 15:16).

I am a personal, Spirit-empowered witness of Christ (Acts 1:8).

I am a temple of God (1 Cor. 3:16).

I am a minister of reconciliation for God (2 Cor. 5:17-21).

I am God's coworker (2 Cor. 6:1).

I am seated with Christ in the heavenly realm (Eph. 2:6).

I am God's workmanship, created for good works (Eph. 2:10).

I may approach God with freedom and confidence (Eph. 3:12).

I can do all things through Christ who strengthens me! (Phil. 4:13).

By the grace of God, I am what I am (1 Cor. 15:10).[1]

Knowing that our sins are forgiven and that we have new life in Christ leads us to the last third of the gospel, which is often overlooked in American culture. John offers another explanation why Jesus came. "The reason the Son of God appeared was to destroy the devil's work" (1 John 3:8). When I travel in Third World countries, this is the part of the gospel people are waiting to hear. In their pagan practices they have been trying to appease the deities (demons) with sacrifices and peace offerings, and they have been trying to manipulate the spiritual world through shamans and witch doctors. Knowing that the devil is defeated and that every believer has authority over the kingdom of darkness is just as much a part of the gospel as the fact that our sins are forgiven. Notice how Paul puts the whole gospel together in Colossians 2:13-15:

> **KNOWING THAT THE DEVIL IS DEFEATED AND THAT EVERY BELIEVER HAS AUTHORITY OVER THE KINGDOM OF DARKNESS IS JUST AS MUCH A PART OF THE GOSPEL AS THE FACT THAT OUR SINS ARE FORGIVEN.**

When you were dead in your sins and in the uncircumcision of your sinful nature, God made you alive with Christ. He forgave us all our sins, having canceled the written code, with its regulations, that was against us and that stood opposed to us; he took it away, nailing it to the cross. And having disarmed the powers and authorities, he made a public spectacle of them, triumphing over them by the cross.

If you were the devil and you wanted to disrupt the plans of God and cause conflict within the Body of Christ, what would you do? First, you would try to divide the mind of the believers, because double-minded people are unstable in all their ways (see Jas. 1:8). Listen to the warning of Paul: "The Spirit clearly says that in later times some will abandon the faith and follow deceiving spirits and things taught by demons" (1 Tim. 4:1; see also 2 Cor. 11:3). We are seeing evidence of that happening all over the world as we work with people. Believing lies not only destroys their faith but also causes numerous conflicts in their marriages and ministries.

Second, you would try to divide a marriage, because a house divided against itself cannot stand (see Matt. 12:25). Marriage and family are the building blocks of every society, and they are under siege. No society can be any better than its families, and the same holds true for the Church. If your church has many unhealthy marriages, you have a unhealthy church. If the people in your church are not experiencing their freedom in Christ, you have unhealthy marriages and a unhealthy church. The whole cannot be any greater than the sum of its parts.

Finally, you would try to divide the Body of Christ, because any kingdom divided against itself cannot stand, but any kingdom united together with one purpose will stand. Scripture teaches that we are to be single-minded, become one in our marriages and have unity in the body of Christ, and that can only happen if we are living free "in Christ."[2]

If spiritual warfare is new to you, then maybe you can identify with my experience. I was an aerospace engineer before I became a Christian. I thought science was the answer and believed there was a natural explanation for everything. Then I became a Christian and enrolled in a good seminary. I learned about the kingdom of God but was taught little about the kingdom of darkness. I learned how to explain almost every human problem on the basis of the world and the flesh but not the devil. Armed with a seminary degree, I became a pastor. I believed that Christ was the answer and that the truth of His Word would set people free, but I really did not know how.

The Lord started bringing people to me who had severe problems, and I tried as best I could to help them. I would share Scripture and pray, but I saw little change in the way people behaved. While pastoring, I had a man in my church who was the source of many conflicts. One day he told me that he had a voice in his head that plagued him with foul, blasphemous and accusing thoughts. Was he mentally ill or under spiritual attack? I suspected the latter, but I was not sure, and even if he were under attack, I would not have known what to do about it at that time. So he remained in bondage, and the conflicts within his home and our church remained.

I have since gone through a lot of paradigm shifts in my thinking and understanding of this world and the Word of God. I now believe that the essential battle from Genesis to Revelation is between the kingdom of God and the kingdom of darkness, between Christ and Satan, between good and evil, between the spirit of truth and the father of lies, between the true prophets and the false prophets. Paul taught that, "Our struggle is not against flesh and blood, but against the rulers, against the powers, against the world forces of this darkness, against the spiritual forces of wickedness in the heavenly places" (Eph. 6:12, *NASB*). Consequently, every Christian needs to put on the armor of God and be "on the alert with all perseverance and petition for *all* the saints" (v. 18, *NASB*, emphasis added). Peter admonished us, "Be of sober spirit, be on the alert. Your adversary, the devil, prowls about like a roaring lion, seeking someone to devour" (1 Pet. 5:8, *NASB*).

Understanding conflict and seeking the right solution require a biblical worldview, and that requires an understanding of the spiritual battle that is going on in the heavenlies, the spiritual realm. Jesus called Satan the ruler of this world (see John 14:30), and Satan has deceived the whole world (see Rev. 12:9). John taught that, "The whole world lies in the power of the evil one" (1 John 5:19, *NASB*). Concerning this world and those who are unsaved, Paul wrote, "the god of this world has blinded the minds [*noema*] of the unbelieving, that they might not see the light of the gospel of the glory of Christ, who is the image of God" (2 Cor. 4:4, *NASB*).

On a personal level, Paul admonished us to forgive so "that no advantage be taken of us by Satan; for we are not ignorant of his schemes [*noema*]" (2 Cor. 2:11, *NASB*). Many Christians are languishing in bitterness, and Satan has taken advantage of their unwillingness to forgive. Consequently, there is no possibility for reconciliation with others. In my early years of ministry, I was ignorant of Satan's schemes, how he influences our thoughts. The word "noema" is usually translated as "mind" or "thought" and is only used six times in Scripture. In 2 Corinthians 10:5 (*NASB*), Paul wrote, "We are destroying speculations and every lofty thing raised up against the knowledge of God, and we are taking every thought [noema] captive to the obedience of Christ." If a thought comes to your mind that is not true, then do not believe it. But it is not enough to stop thinking negative thoughts; we have to choose the truth. Paul admonishes us to bring our anxious thoughts to God, "And the peace of God, which surpasses all comprehension, shall guard your hearts and your minds (noema) in Christ Jesus" (Phil. 4:7, *NASB*). If we do not win this battle for our minds, there will be personal defeat and interpersonal conflicts.

To resolve personal and interpersonal conflicts, we need to submit to God and resist the devil (see Jas. 4:7). Trying to resist the devil without first submitting to God will result in a "dog-fight." Taking on the devil in the flesh is not advisable, but Satan has no power or authority over a child of God who is seated with Christ in the heavenlies and filled with the Holy Spirit. On the other hand, you can submit to God, fail to resist the devil and stay in conflict. We need the whole gospel, for it is only the gospel in its entirety that takes into account all reality, as the following testimony illustrates:

> In 1993, I purchased a set of your tapes. After listening to these tapes, I began applying the principles to my individual problems. I realized that some of them could be spiritual attacks, and I learned how to take a stand and, as a result, won victories over some challenges in my life.
>
> But this is only the tip of the iceberg. I'm a deacon and a preacher in a Baptist church. The pastor of my church had suffered from depression and other problems that I was not aware of, and in 1994 he committed suicide. This literally brought our church to its knees. Thinking back over some of the problems facing the previous pastors, I felt the source of the trouble was spiritual. But I did not know how to relay this to the congregation, since we had been taught that the devil or a demon cannot affect a Christian.
>
> The church elected me as their interim pastor. While in a local bookstore, I saw your book *Setting Your Church*

Free. I purchased it and read it. Considering the spiritual oppression in our church, I believed the material you presented was our answer. The only problem was getting the rest of the church to agree. After a few weeks of preaching on spiritual attack and deliverance, I knew that we had to go through the process of setting our church free, just as you outlined in that book.

Slowly, very slowly, the people accepted that teaching and I was able to contact one of your staff for help. This man flew to our city and led the leaders of our church through the "Steps to Setting Your Church Free." The leaders loved it! I felt step one was past, and we were ready to move ahead.

I wanted to take the congregation through the individual "Steps to Freedom in Christ." Six weeks later, I was able to do so. I really don't understand how it all happened, but I can say that we were set free from the spiritual bondage of multiple problems. I would have to write a book in order to explain all that took place.

During this time, one of the middle-aged members, who happened to be an evangelist, was set free. He learned who he was in Christ and is back in the ministry—praise the Lord. I saw the twin daughters of the deceased pastor set free and able to forgive their father. These girls were able to go on with their lives in victory, even though at one point one of them had contemplated suicide too.

We have a new church; God is free to work here! We founded a pulpit committee, and our church voted unanimously to hire our current pastor. That had never happened before.

Well, when you do things God's way, you get God's results.

In His high priestly prayer, Jesus said, "My prayer is not that you take them out of the world but that you protect them from the evil one. They are not of the world, even as I am not of it. Sanctify them by the truth; your word is truth" (John 17:15-16). Jesus is the truth, and the Holy Spirit is the Spirit of truth; He will lead us into all truth, and that truth will set us free. However, the devil is the father of lies. If we believe his lies, then we will stay in bondage and live defeated lives. Jesus had another concern in His prayer—future believers. "My prayer is not for them alone [His disciples]. I pray also for those who will believe in me through their message, that all of them may be one, Father, just as you are in me and I am in you. May they also be in us so that the world may believe that you have sent me" (vv. 20-21).

What is the basis for our unity? Is it common physical heritage? Of course not, because we could never be united given our ethnic diversity. Besides, even family members fight like cats and dogs. Is it common doctrine? Again, I would have to say no, because even spouses do hold to the exact same theology all the time. Although we should strive for doctrinal purity, it is unlikely that we will ever agree upon every point of doctrine. We do not have to have unanimity or uniformity in order to have unity. We do not have to perfectly agree in order to live in harmony with one another, as any married couple living in peace has discovered. The basis for our unity is a common spiritual heritage. Every believer is a child of God. We are brothers and sisters in Christ. We are all uniquely different, but we share the same Father, have the same Spirit within us and read the same Bible. The unity of the Spirit is within us, as Paul teaches in Ephesians 4:2-6:

Be completely humble and gentle; be patient, bearing with one another in love. Make every effort to keep the unity of the Spirit through the bond of peace. There is one body and one Spirit—just as you were called to one hope when you were called—one Lord, one faith, one baptism; one God and Father of all, who is over all and through all and in all.

CHAPTER 3

ONE NEW MAN

Ephesians 2:11-22

When the rams are following their shepherd and looking to him, their woolies rub each other companionably; but when they look at one another they see only each other's horns.

Z. A. Salik, *Living Quotations for Christians*

It was November 7, 1980. I (Neil) was taking my last doctoral class at Pepperdine University. On my way to class that evening, I was listening to the election results on the car radio at 7:30 P.M. President Jimmy Carter was giving his concession speech a half hour before the polls closed in California. It was also apparent that the Senate had gone Republican for the first time in years. I was elated to see the political pendulum swing more to the right, but I was not prepared for the mood of the class when I arrived.

I had tried to petition out of this class on cultural pluralism on the basis that I had taken seminary classes on missions and anthropology. How thankful I am that my attempts had failed. The class consisted primarily of educational administrators and teachers who were all working on their doctorates. They were sharp people who had their fingers on the pulse of our society. In this class I was completely in the minority in race, religion and gender. Of the 23 students, I was probably the only evangelical Christian—at least the only one who would identify himself as such. Sensing the mood of the class that evening, I thought it would be wise to keep my mouth shut and listen.

My enthusiasm for the political shift was quickly dampened by the rest of the class, who considered the movement to the right to be a setback to the causes they had given their lives for. They were afraid that the collective voice of the minorities was going to be drowned out again by the majority. Looking back, I do not think their fears were totally realized, but I thank God for the experience of listening to those who had not had the same privileges that I have enjoyed. There are a lot of socioeconomic forces promoting discrimination, but it's important to realize that at its root, it is not a corporate problem—it is a personal problem. Culture changes one person at a time. I had to ask myself, *Did I want every newly born child in America to have the same opportunity as my children? Would I be willing to commit a portion of my time and resources to ensure that happens? As a minimum, would I be willing to speak up or take action when I hear or see social injustices taking place?* If I could not answer in the affirmative, then I was part of the problem, not part of the answer. Reconciliation is costly, because there is no fence-sitting.

When I finished the class, I was a little more mature than when I had enrolled, but not just because I had had the experience of being in the minority—my experience lasted for a semester, theirs for a lifetime. I was impacted by their perspective on racism, equal opportunity and the injustices of our society. Most of what they shared, I had never experienced. So why would I want to change a system that favors me? Why give up my comfortable conformity to work for the rights of others? Why sacrifice my time, talent and treasure for the needs of others? Because Jesus did! He reigns in my heart, and I want to be like Him. If our desire is to be like Him, then according to Philippians 2:3-5 (*NASB*) we should:

Do nothing from selfishness or empty conceit, but with humility of mind let each of you regard one another as more important than himself; do not merely look out for your own personal interests, but also for the interests of others. Have this attitude in yourselves which was also in Christ Jesus.

I was raised in Lutheran country, where the Catholics were the minority. Racism was playful bantering between the Norwegians and the Swedes! I did not see a person with skin pigmentation different from my own until I was 12 years old, when my family made a trip from the farm to Minneapolis. I recall singing in my all-white church, "Red and yellow, black and white, we are precious in His sight." I never realized that red, yellow and black children were treated any differently from the way I was in this land of opportunity. Later, as the civil rights movement was gaining momentum in the early '60s, I was in the Navy, and I saw the struggle of racism for the first time. Although progress is being made, the American culture is far from where it should be.

Thankfully, the kingdom of God is not like the exclusive social societies of our world. The inclusive nature of God is clearly taught in Scripture; the Church, however, has not always modeled it. Martin Luther King, Jr., said of the Church in America,

It is still true that the Church is the most segregated major institution in America. As a minister of the gospel I am ashamed to have to affirm that eleven o'clock on Sunday morning, when we stand to sing, "In Christ There Is No East Nor West," is the most segregated hour of America, and the Sunday School is the most segregated school of the week.[1]

As ministers of the gospel, Chuck and I are ashamed to admit that the Church was not the primary force behind the civil rights movement. It was the state that initiated the process of integration, and it was even opposed by some who professed to be Christians. The founding fathers of our great nation declared that all men are created equal, and they got that understanding from the Bible.

It is even more tragic when some in the Church twist the Scriptures in order to condone genocide, slavery, racism, sexism and classism. Some saw the settling of America as the "conquest of Canaan," thereby justifying the slaughter of Native Americans. Did you know that approximately 10 million Native Americans were killed in this "conquest of Canaan"? Others have used the supposed curses of Cain and Ham to support slavery and racism. Never mind the fact that the descendants of Cain did not survive the flood and that Ham never was cursed.[2] The same twisted logic is being used to support white supremacy in the United States and Western Europe. Many of the Dutch Reformed churches supported apartheid in South Africa. Somehow they justified a policy of segregation and political and economic discrimination against non-European groups. Mohandas Gandhi rejected Christianity because he was refused entrance into a South African church where a friend of his was preaching.[3] Christianity is seldom rejected in its purity, but it is often rejected when perverted by its followers.

Some religious leaders have even blamed the Jews for killing Jesus, when Scripture clearly teaches that it was Pontius Pilate, a Roman governor, who ordered the execution, and it was carried out by Roman soldiers. The twisted cross of Nazism led to the slaughter of 6 million Jews during World War II, but anti-Semitism has been around a lot longer than that. Others have suppressed the role of women, believing that Eve was the cause of the fall, when Scripture teaches that she was deceived, and it was Adam who sinned.

All this justification and rationalization, even in light of the fact that "there is no distinction between Greek and Jew, circumcised and uncircumcised, barbarian, Scythian, slave and freeman, but Christ is all, and in all" (Col. 3:11, *NASB*). Paul adds in Galatians 3:28, "There is neither male nor female; for you are all one in Christ Jesus." In other words, for all those who throw themselves upon the mercy of God, there are no racial, religious, cultural, social or sexual distinctions among those who are graciously entitled children of God. Every born-again believer has the same spiritual heritage.

When Paul won a runaway slave to Christ, he sent him back to his master and instructed Philemon to receive the runaway as a brother and to accept him "as you would me" (Philem. 1:17, *NASB*). Peter instructed every husband to grant his wife honor "as a fellow heir of the grace of life" (1 Pet. 3:7, *NASB*). We may not have the same callings in life, but we are each to be treated as a child of God and given equal status in the Body of Christ. Gordon Allport wrote:

> We have seen that [religion] may be of an ethnocentric order, aiding and abetting a lifestyle marked by prejudice and exclusiveness. Or it may be of a universalistic order, vitally distilling ideals of brotherhood into thought and conduct. Thus we cannot speak sensibly of the relation between religion and prejudice without specifying the sort of religion we mean and the role it plays in the personal life.[4]

WILL THE REAL JESUS PLEASE COME FORWARD?

Does Christianity in its pure form support a faith of prejudice and divisiveness or a faith that nurtures reconciliation and inclusion? Have we twisted Scripture to accommodate our own prejudices and selfish ambitions? Have we been placated by our childhood fantasies of a passive Jesus who strikes a resemblance to Santa Claus? Writing about the Jesus he never knew, Philip Yancey says, "How is it, then, that the Church has tamed such a character—has, in Dorothy Sayer's words, 'very efficiently pared the claws of the Lion of Judah, certified Him as a fitting household pet for pale curates and pious ladies?'"[5] Jesus was always loving, but He never catered to religious hypocrisy, discrimination and social injustices.

The real Jesus is clearly revealed in the Bible, but it is humanly impossible to fully comprehend Him because of our limited perspectives, prejudices and biased educational experiences. We need the inspiration of the Holy Spirit to fully comprehend the true nature of Jesus. Curtiss Paul DeYoung wrote,

> Perhaps this is the greatest challenge to reconciliation: the dividing wall erected by varied perceptions of Jesus, each of which has created its own faith understanding. . . . As we observe the modern-day representation of Jesus, we must ask, "Which Jesus is the real Jesus?" The Jesus of the Democrats or the Jesus of the Republicans? The Jesus of Billy Graham or the Jesus of Jesse Jackson? The Jesus of Mother Teresa or the Jesus of Madonna? The rich Jesus or the poor Jesus? The Protestant Jesus or the Catholic Jesus? The Baptist Jesus or the Methodist Jesus? The black Jesus or the white Jesus? The Asian Jesus or the Native American Jesus? The high church Jesus or the holy roller Jesus? The urban Jesus or the suburban Jesus? Jesus Christ the superstar or Jesus Christ the suffering servant? The Jesus portrayed in stained glass windows or the Jesus in The heart of blood-stained victims of violence?[6]

So critical is this issue of reconciliation with God and others, that I thought it best to quote all of Paul's prominent teaching in Ephesians 2:11-21:

> Therefore, remember that formerly you who are Gentiles by birth and called "uncircumcised" by those who call themselves "the circumcision" (that done in the body by the hands of men)—remember that at that time you were separate from Christ, excluded from citizenship in Israel and foreigners to the covenants of the promise, without hope and without God in the world. But now in Christ Jesus you who once were far away have been brought near through the blood of Christ.
>
> For he himself is our peace, who has made the two one and has destroyed the barrier, the dividing wall of hostility, by abolishing in his flesh the law with its commandments and regulations. His purpose was to create in himself one new man out of the two, thus making peace, and in this one body to reconcile both of them to God through the cross, by which he put to death their hostility. He came and preached peace to you who were far away and peace to those who were near. For through him we both have access to the Father by one Spirit.
>
> Consequently, you are no longer foreigners and aliens, but fellow citizens with God's people and members of God's household, built on the foundation of the apostles and prophets, with Christ Jesus himself as the chief cornerstone.

THE CURTAIN WAS TORN

The "wall of hostility" (Eph. 2:14) refers to the barrier that divided the inner and outer courts of the Jewish temple. The outer racial, cultural and social barriers in the court of the Gentiles were removed (i.e., no distinction between barbarian, Scythian, slave and free).

For those who do not believe, the veil remains in place. Paul cites two specific cases where this is true. First, the veil is effective for those who choose to live under the Law and relate only to the Old Covenant.

> For to this day the same veil remains when the old covenant is read. It has not been removed, because only in Christ is it taken away. Even to this day when Moses is read, a veil covers their hearts. But whenever anyone turns to the Lord, the veil is taken away (2 Cor. 3:14-15).

Reconciliation will never be effective by living under the Law. Legalistic attempts at reconciliation do not work, for the law kills, but the Spirit gives life (see 2 Cor. 3:6). Reconciliation is spiritual work, and it requires the enabling power of the Holy Spirit. We know we are reconciled to God when His Spirit bears witness with our spirit that we are children of God (see Rom. 8:16). We are reconciled to others because of the spiritual union every believer has in Christ. It becomes effective in our experience when we have forgiven one another and repented of our sins.

The fact that reconciliation is a spiritual work is evident in revivals, which are a work of the Holy Spirit. When the Spirit moves upon people, they spontaneously repent of their sins and are moved to reconcile with their brothers and sisters in Christ. Nobody has to tell them to do that; they are compelled by the Holy Spirit to forgive and seek forgiveness. I heard Vance Havner, a well-known pastor and evangelist, say, "When the spiritual tide is out, every little tadpole wants his own little tide pool to swim in. But when the spiritual tide is in, they all swim with one accord."

court was the court of the Gentiles. In Scripture, a Gentile is an one who is not a Jew. Gentiles were the "uncircumcised" and t furthest removed from the holy of holies. Paul was imprison in Rome when he wrote the above words to the church Ephesus. Ironically, he had been falsely charged for bringing Gentile into the inner courts of the Temple (see Acts 21:27-29 Jewish women could go into the next court in the Temple, bu only the Jewish men could proceed into the holy place. In th court, the priests performed their sacrifices according to the Law. But only the high priest could go from the holy place to the most holy place, and he could go only once a year, to make atonement for all the sins of Israel. A veil separated God from His Chosen People.

MORE THAN THE CURTAIN FELL THAT DAY—SO DID EVERY BARRIER IN THE TEMPLE. THERE WAS NO LONGER ANY SEPARATION BETWEEN THE MOST HOLY PLACE AND THE HOLY PLACE.

Then came that fateful afternoon when "the sun stopped shining. And the curtain of the temple was torn in two" (Luke 23:45). How they must have trembled in the Temple as the veil was removed the moment Christ died for all our sins. More than the curtain fell that day. So did every barrier in the Temple. There was no longer any separation between the most holy place and the holy place to which all the Jewish men had access. The barrier between the Jewish men and women was torn down, as was the division between the Jew and the Gentile. "There is neither Jew nor Greek, slave nor free, male nor female, for you are all one in Christ Jesus" (Gal. 3:28). Even the

I witnessed this in a remarkable conference in the Philippines. I was told before I went that there were many factions in the Body of Christ. I did not try to mend fences; I told them about who they are in Christ and how to resolve their personal and spiritual issues. After helping them do that by taking them through the Steps to Freedom in Christ, a revival broke out. Those dear saints worshiped together as one in Christ, and in the midst of the celebration they were moved to forgive one another and set aside their differences.

It has become a popular notion to believe that theology is divisive. I disagree; intellectual arrogance is divisive. If we are theologically astute, then we should know that "knowledge puffs up, but love builds up" (1 Cor. 8:1). Intellectually arrogant people are often the hardest to reconcile with others, and they are seldom known for their love. Theological elitists can be divisive, even if they are biblically correct. They have captured the letter of the Law but not the Spirit of the Law. If our theology is correct, and we believe it, it should cause us to fall in love with God and each other. "All the Law and the Prophets hang on these two commandments" (Matt. 22:40). In other words, God's inspired Word was given so that by knowing God we may fall in love with Him and our neighbors. "The goal of this command is love" (1 Tim. 1:5).

> **IF OUR THEOLOGY IS CORRECT, AND WE BELIEVE IT, IT SHOULD CAUSE US TO FALL IN LOVE WITH GOD AND EACH OTHER.**

Second, the devil does not want us to know the truth that will set us free. "If our gospel is veiled, it is veiled to those who are perishing. The god of this age has blinded the minds of unbelievers, so that they cannot see the light of the gospel of the glory of Christ, who is the image of God" (2 Cor. 4:3-4). The first strategy of Satan is to keep us from coming to Christ. If that should fail, he does not curl up his tail and pull in his fangs. His second strategy is to keep us from understanding the full gospel. He cannot do anything about our position in Christ, but if he can deceive us into thinking that what the Bible has to say about who were are in Christ is not true, then we will live as though it is not true. The Early Church father Irenaeus wrote:

> The devil, however, as he is the apostate angel, can only go to this length, as he did at the beginning, to deceive and lead astray the mind of man into disobeying the commandments of God, and gradually to darken the hearts.[7]

ONE NEW MAN

Several years ago I was leading a conference at a refugee center in Croatia during the war there. The facilities allowed us to accommodate only 50 evangelical pastors in this predominantly Catholic country. I quickly observed that every pastor present was depressed. This was due partly to the ravages of war, but I began to realize that Communism had also stripped them of any sense of self. It was as if they had no individual identity and they believed they were nothing but sinners waiting for the judgment hammer of God to fall (some thought it was falling). I told them: The hammer of God has already fallen. It fell on Christ when He died once for all. They were not sinners in the hands of an angry God; they were saints in the hands of a loving God who has called them to come before His presence "with freedom and confidence" (Eph. 3:12). They were not children of the state, they were children of God—and they began to believe it. After four days an oppressive cloud had lifted, and they knew that their identity in Christ was the only answer for their country after the war.

Since the Fall, any attempt to unify humanity apart from Christ has failed. Communism held Yugoslavia together by sheer force under the rule of Marshal Tito. As soon as the external yoke of Communism was thrown off, the country splintered into Slovenia, Croatia, Bosnia and Serbia. Those ethnic and religious identities had been around for nearly 1,000 years. Nothing external could change that. Even the Body of Christ becomes divided when we seek our identity in something other than Christ. Sectarianism, individualism and even denominationalism will keep us separated and less effective than if we cooperated and worked together. I am not talking about the old ecumenicalism that got watered down in liberalism and therefore offered no real basis for unity. I am talking about the true Body of Christ, in which each member is "joined together . . . to become a holy temple . . . built together to become a dwelling in which God lives by his Spirit" (Eph. 2:21-22).

Remember the passage quoted earlier? "His purpose was to create in himself one new man out of the two, thus making peace, and in this one body to reconcile both of them to God through the cross" (Eph. 2:15-16). God not only clothes us with Christ, He also makes us a new, unified humanity. When we come to Christ personally, we find ourselves one with all others "in Him." Paul wrote, "You are all one in Christ Jesus" (Gal. 3:28, *NASB*) and "we are members of one another" (Eph. 4:25, *NASB*).

Have we emphasized a personal relationship with God at the expense of a corporate relationship with Him? Has our English language, that has no plural "you," contributed to that? We think Scripture is addressing us as individuals when it is actually addressing the whole Body of Christ. God never designed us to grow in isolation from other believers. It was His intention from the beginning that we grow together as a community. God's declaration before the Fall, "It is not good for the man to be alone" (Gen. 2:18, *NASB*), is related to growth as much as any other part of human life. Sanctification is not just a matter of *I* or *me*. It is more commonly understood as *we* and *us*.

> ## GOD NEVER DESIGNED US TO GROW IN ISOLATION FROM OTHER BELIEVERS. IT WAS HIS INTENTION FROM THE BEGINNING THAT WE GROW TOGETHER AS A COMMUNITY.

We cannot have a wholesome relationship with God, nor successfully conform to His image, in isolation from others. Our relationship with God is inextricably bound up in our relationship with the rest of humanity. For instance, the word "saint" is used 60 times in the plural but only once in the singular. Our personal identity in Christ cannot be understood apart from our relationship with other saints. In Western culture, where we emphasize individuality, we often surmise that individuality and sharing in a group are opposed—that our individuality is lost when we become part of a group. In actuality, the opposite is true. We gain our true selfhood by sharing in community. Ernest Wright explains this basic concept:

> To belong to community is to share the life of a "people," and the conception of "people" arose from the understanding of starting in the father's household, extending to the family, and finally to all kinsmen who take part in the whole of the common history.[8]

Peter emphasizes this identification of ourselves as a people when he wrote, "You are a chosen people, a royal priesthood, a holy nation, a people belonging to God, that you may declare the praises of him who called you out of darkness into his wonderful light. Once you were not a people, but now you are the people of God; once you had not received mercy, but now you have received mercy" (1 Pet. 2:9-10). We exist, then, not as separate entities, but as part of humanity. We cannot live the life for which we were created if we live in isolation from the rest of humanity. As the Danish scholar Pedersen wrote,

> All life is common life ... no soul can live an isolated life. It is not only that it cannot get along without the assistance of others; it is in direct conflict with its essence to be apart. It can only exist as a link of a whole, and it cannot work or act without working in connection with other souls and through them.[9]

Our personal individuality—who we really are—comes only in relation to others: God, our family and our fellow believers. Old Testament scholar L. Kohler said, "Ein mensch ist kein mensch" (One man is no man).[10] We absolutely need God, and we necessarily need each other. Our divine purpose is not fully realized apart from Christian community, and sin disrupts that. When we choose to live independent of God, we not only alienate ourselves from the creator, but also from our brothers and sisters in Christ. Even secular psychologists like Eric Fromm have observed the destructiveness of such separation and the need for fellowship.

> Man is gifted with reason: he is life being aware of itself; he has awareness of himself, of his fellow man, of his past, and of the possibilities of his future. This awareness of himself as a separate entity, the awareness of his own short life span, of the fact that without his will he is

born and against his will he dies, that he will die before those whom he loves, or they before him, the awareness of his aloneness and separateness, of his helplessness before the forces of nature and of society, all this makes his separate, disunited existence an unbearable prison. He would become insane could he not liberate himself from this prison and reach out, unite himself in some form or other with men, with the world outside.[11]

If we require community to know fulfillment as children of God, then reconciliation with our brothers and sisters in Christ is necessary for our sanctification. We are not perfect people, and we do not live with perfect people. Experiencing oneness requires us to continue the struggle against the sin that alienates us. As we shall learn later, forgiveness is the Christian way of life. We cannot change another person, but we can change ourselves by the grace of God. Nobody can keep us from being the people God created us to be, which is God's will for our lives. We are bound together in Christ for all eternity, so it is imperative that we learn to live with one another in a gracious way.

CHAPTER 4

IN THE HOPE THAT GOD WILL GRANT REPENTANCE

2 Timothy 2:24-26

Man is born with his back toward God. When he truly repents, he turns right around and faces God. Repentance is a change of mind. . . . Repentance is the tear in the eye of faith.

D. L. Moody

I (Neil) was conducting a one-day seminar in what appeared to be a very successful church. The plan called for me to come back in nine months to do a full conference. The church seemed healthy and had grown significantly under its pastor of more than 20 years. But as I soon discovered on my second visit, this significant ministry was on the road to self-destruction. My wife and I could sense an oppressive spirit even before we reached the facilities. In the preceding months, the youth pastor had successfully undermined the ministry of the senior pastor, and both had resigned under fire. All my available time that week was spent meeting with different factions of the church. The board and staff were split down the middle. Some blamed the senior pastor, and others blamed the youth pastor.

During the course of the week, I heard from the interim pastor that the board and staff were going to have a meeting on Thursday evening, the night I was going to teach about forgiveness. I recommended that they change the meeting to Friday evening, the only night of the week that our conference on resolving personal and spiritual conflicts was not meeting. I invited all of them to hear the message on forgiveness, and I offered to meet with them on Friday evening if they so desired. They agreed. The newly appointed interim pastor was asked to chair a committee that would investigate the nature of the conflict and make recommendations to the board. I thought that was ill advised, since the pastor was a good shepherd and a healer of relationships. He would serve the church better if he stayed neutral and available to everyone. He agreed with me, and we approached the denominational leader to see if he would chair the committee instead. He also agreed, and so did the board when we met that Friday evening.

You did not have to be a spiritual giant to sense the tension that Friday evening. Having met the various participants during personal appointments that week, I could see that the two factions were sitting on opposite sides of the table. I had been praying all day, "Lord, what can I do in this one meeting?" Not only did I feel helpless, but I was also physically exhausted from speaking all week and conducting many private counseling sessions. Plus, I had to speak all day Saturday. I knew I was not the answer, but I did know that God was the answer and their only hope.

I began the evening by telling them of a book I had read years ago entitled *Then Came Jesus.*[1] The author told of different episodes in his life when Jesus had provided the only way out. Even if the appointed committee were successful in finding out who the culprits were and what had caused the conflicts in the first place, that alone would not solve their problems. Establishing blame never does, and, in this case, the two personalities who were at the center of the controversy were gone. Obviously, the departure of the pastors had not resolved the conflicts in the church either. Assuming that the dismissal of the pastors was justified, it was now the responsibility of the leadership to ensure that Jesus was in the center of their own personal lives and ministries.

I started the evening by recalling the biblical story of Jesus feeding the 5,000 (see Mark 6:33-44). The Lord told His disciples to give food to the crowd who had gathered to hear Him teach, but they responded, "That would take eight months of a man's wages! Are we to go and spend that much on bread and give it to them to eat?" (v. 37). Their response reveals the same human tendency that plagues the Church today. When confronted by what seems to be an impossible task given to us by the Lord, we think only of our own resources. We will never bear fruit if we try to do the Lord's work in our own strength and resources. Jesus took what they had—five loaves and two fish—divided it up and fed them all. The disciples gathered up what was left, and they each had their own basket of food (see v. 43). What an object lesson!

> **THE NUMBER-ONE OBSTACLE FOR THE MINISTRY OF RECONCILIATION IS SELF-SUFFICIENCY.**

Then Jesus went away to pray and sent the disciples across the Sea of Galilee. In the middle of the night, they were straining at the oars but not making any progress against the wind. Mark recorded that Jesus, "intended to pass by them" (v. 48, *NASB*) as He walked across the sea at night. Jesus intends to pass by the self-sufficient.

If we want to row against the storms of life, we can do it, and Jesus will let us row until our arms fall off. Or we can call upon the Lord and He will save us. The number-one obstacle for the ministry of reconciliation is self-sufficiency. The church was in the midst of a storm, and the leaders' task was to ensure that Jesus was in the boat with them.

I continued by saying, "In a moment, I am going to pray. Afterward I would like a few minutes of individual silent prayer as you consider the following four questions: How am I a part of the problem? How can I be a part of the solution? Whom do I need to forgive? Whom do I need to seek forgiveness from?" Several minutes went by and "then came Jesus" (see v. 48) Several confessed, "Lord, I don't want to be self-sufficient and part of the problem." Many confessed their own sins. The wind died down. Finally the interim pastor prayed, "Thank You, Lord, that You didn't pass us by tonight." Although it was a "God moment," I would suspect that some were still like the disciples who had not learned the lesson from the feeding of the 5,000 because "their hearts were hardened" (v. 52).

Before I left that evening, I told them one more boat story. This time Jesus was in the boat and sound asleep as the disciples were struggling against the storm (see Mark 4:35-41). They woke Him up and said, "Teacher, don't you care if we drown?" (v. 38). After rebuking the wind, Jesus said to His disciples, "Why are you so afraid? Do you still have no faith?" (v. 40). I said to these dear saints, "Do you really think your boat will sink if Jesus is in it? If Jesus is in the boat with you, He will get you across to the other side. Just make sure He is in the boat."

Believing that all conflicts will be resolved if only the problem person or people would leave is a mistake that many churches

make. People have taken sides, and bitterness has taken root in many lives. The ministry of reconciliation requires all involved to repent, forgive those who have offended them and seek the forgiveness of those they have offended. First and foremost, our need to repent and forgive others is an issue between ourselves and God. Even if we are purely victims, we still need to forgive those who have offended us if we want to live free in Christ. In most cases, we are not entirely without fault, and that needs to be acknowledged, even if the other person is the primary cause of the conflict. Reconciliation can only happen if we are right with God. Jesus said:

> Why do you look at the speck of sawdust in your brother's eye and pay no attention to the plank in your own eye? How can you say to your brother, "Let me take the speck out of your eye," when all the time there is a plank in your own eye? You hypocrite, first take the plank out of your own eye, and then you will see clearly to remove the speck from your brother's eye (Matt. 7:3-5).

In order to be reconciled with others, we have to first be fully reconciled with God. The tool we use to accomplish this is the Steps to Freedom in Christ.[2] The purpose of these steps is to resolve any issues that are blocking us from having an intimate relationship with God. To experience His presence we have to submit to God and resist the devil, who may have taken advantage of the doorways that we have left open for him. We believe that repentance will be complete if we will deal with the following seven issues that are critical between ourselves and God.

COUNTERFEIT VERSUS REAL

In making a public profession of faith, converts in the Early Church would stand, face the west and say, "I renounce you,

Satan, and all your works and all your ways." This was the first step in repentance. The Catholic church and most liturgical churches still require that to be said at baptism and confirmation. This is now a generic statement, however. The converts in the Early Church would specifically renounce every counterfeit religious experience they had had, every false vow or pledge they had made and every false teacher or doctrine which they had believed. We encourage every person we counsel to do that as well. To renounce means to give up a claim or a right. To "renounce" means that we are making a definite decision to let go of the past commitments, pledges, vows, pacts and beliefs that are not Christian. "He who conceals his sins does not prosper, but whoever confesses and renounces them finds mercy" (Prov. 28:13).

Some people commit themselves to Christ and choose to believe the Word of God but still hold on to past commitments and beliefs. They just add something on to what they already had—and their reconciliation with God is incomplete. Every believer must decisively let go of the past, which is the first step of genuine repentance. If we understand and embrace what is true, then we should also understand and reject what is not true. All this was made possible because of Christ's crucifixion and resurrection. Our sins are forgiven and we have new life in Christ the moment we are born again, but our minds are not instantly renewed. There is no "clear" button in our mental computers. Everything that was programmed into our minds before Christ is still there. That is why Paul wrote: "Do not conform any longer to the pattern of this world, but be transformed by the renewing of your mind" (Rom. 12:2). That is repentance.

Paul links repentance and truth together: "We have renounced secret and shameful ways; we do not use deception, nor do we distort the word of God" (2 Cor. 4:2). Paul is contrasting the truth of divine revelation with that of false teachers and prophets.

God does not take lightly false guidance and false teachers. In Old Testament times, they were to be stoned to death, and there were serious consequences for those who consulted them. "I will set my face against the person who turns to mediums and spiritists to prostitute himself by following them, and I will cut him off from his people" (Lev. 20:6). There are similar warnings about false teachers and false prophets in the New Testament. That is why we have found it necessary to renounce any and all involvement with false guidance, false teachers, false prophets and every cultic and occultic practice. We do not want to be cut off from God; we want to be fully reconciled to Him.

For example, consider Bill's experience. Following a decision for Christ, he experienced continued difficulty with anger and physical abuse in his marriage. Although he felt convicted about his poor relationship with his wife, he could not seem to stop his aggressive behavior. He was led through the Steps to Freedom at his church. During the process, Bill confessed to using a Ouija board, embracing New Age beliefs and engaging in other occult practices in his life prior to conversion. Renouncing every involvement with false teachers and prophets brought tremendous relief to him. He was now able to work constructively on his lifestyle issues, and it was recommended that he read *Getting Anger Under Control* by Neil T. Anderson and Rich Miller.[3] Bill and his wife are communicating much better and are joyfully expecting their first child.

DECEPTION VERSUS TRUTH

We are admonished to speak the truth in love (see Eph. 4:15), walk in the light and have fellowship with one another (see 1 John 1:7). People living in conflict believe lies, walk in darkness and lack or avoid intimate contact with others. Deception is the major strategy of the evil one, because he knows that truth sets us free. If he accused us, we would know it. It he tempted us, we would know it. If he deceived us, we would not know it. How can deception creep in? We can pay attention to deceiving spirits (see 1 Tim. 4:1), believe false prophets and teachers (see 2 Pet. 2:1-10), or we can deceive ourselves in the following ways:

1. Hearing God's word but not doing it (see Jas. 1:22; 4:17)
2. Saying we have no sin (see 1 John 1:8)
3. Thinking we are something when we aren't (see Gal. 6:3)
4. Thinking we are wise in our own eyes (see 1 Cor. 3:18-19)
5. Thinking we will not reap what we sow (see Gal. 6:7)
6. Thinking the unrighteous will inherit the Kingdom (see 1 Cor. 6:9)
7. Thinking we can associate with bad company and not be corrupted (see 1 Cor. 15:33)

The first step toward reconciliation is to admit we have a problem. That means we have to overcome our denial and defense mechanisms. We cannot instantly change long-established flesh patterns that have become a habitual part of our daily lives. But we can make a definitive decision to change the flesh patterns and confess them as wrong. As Christians, we do not have to rely on flimsy defense mechanisms anymore, because we are loved and accepted for who we are. Christ is our defense.

In addition to lying and blaming others, the following defense mechanisms are often hindrances to reconciliation:

1. Denial (conscious or subconscious refusal to face the truth)
2. Fantasy (escaping from the real world)
3. Emotional insulation (withdrawing to avoid rejection)
4. Regression (reverting back to a less-threatening time)

5. Displacement (taking out frustration on others)
6. Projection (attributing our own impulses to someone else)
7. Rationalization (making excuses for poor behavior)

Jody was in a second marriage, and her husband was sexually addicted. And Jody's past had not been much healthier. Her first husband had been verbally abusive. Her mother and father had divorced when she was in elementary school. As a child Jody was allowed to choose the custodial parent. She chose her father, who was frequently absent because he often traveled for work. She essentially raised herself in her father's home, with a neighbor appointed as a guardian during the week. She developed strong defenses of independence, a critical spirit, projection, emotional insulation, denial, complaining and blaming—all of which she had carried into her marriages.

She assumed no responsibility for anything emotional or behavioral in either marriage, adamantly asserting that she had no pain from her childhood or from either marriage. Her sincere belief was that if both of her two husbands could be treated and cured, her problems caused by them would vanish. Consistently, she attempted to control others while clinging to her own self-sufficiency. She was led through the Steps to Freedom in a church ministry, and as a result she was amenable to further counseling and reconciliation. It is unlikely that she would have agreed to that if she had not worked through some of her issues with God.

BITTERNESS VERSUS FORGIVENESS

Reconciliation without forgiveness is impossible. Conflicts leave emotional scars, and many Christians bear the pain of wounds that have been inflicted upon them by others. Most do not know how to let go of the past and forgive from the heart. Some have chosen not to. They hang on to their anger as a means of protecting themselves from being hurt again, but they are only hurting themselves. Through forgiveness we set a captive free—and then discover that *we* were the captives. We cannot be right with God and remain in bitterness. If we do not forgive from our hearts, God will turn us over to the torturers (see Matt. 18:34).

> **RECONCILIATION WITHOUT FORGIVENESS IS IMPOSSIBLE. WE CANNOT BE RIGHT WITH GOD AND REMAIN IN BITTERNESS.**

God is not punishing us; He is disciplining us. He knows that if we hang on to our bitterness, we will only hurt ourselves and others (see Heb. 12:15). Instead, we are to "get rid of all bitterness, rage and anger, brawling and slander, along with every form of malice. Be kind and compassionate to one another, forgiving each other, just as in Christ God forgave you" (Eph. 4:31-32). We forgive others for the sake of our relationship with God. What is to be gained in forgiving others is freedom from our past and the restoration of communion with God. We are also warned by Paul that we need to forgive others so that Satan does not take advantage of us (see 2 Cor. 2:10-11). Forgiveness will be further explained in the next chapter.

REBELLION VERSUS SUBMISSION

We live in a very rebellious age. People think it is their right to criticize and sit in judgment of those who are over them. When sown, the seeds of rebellion reap anarchy and spiritual defeat. If we have a rebellion problem, we have the worst problem in the world. Scripture instructs us to *submit to* and *pray for* those who are in authority over us. Honoring our mother and father is the first of the Ten Commandments that ends in a promise. The same is true in the New Testament:

> Everyone must submit to the governing authorities, for there is no authority except that which God has established. The authorities that exist have been established by God. Consequently, he who rebels against the authority is rebelling against what God has instituted, and those who do so will bring judgment on themselves. For rulers hold no terror for those who do right, but for those who do wrong. Do you want to be free from fear of the one in authority? Then do what is right and he will commend you. For he is God's servant to do you good. But if you do wrong, be afraid, for he does not bear the sword for nothing. He is God's servant, an agent of wrath to bring punishment on the wrongdoer (Rom. 13:1-4).

Imagine the conflict that would have been spared the church if the youth pastor in the opening illustration had been submissive to authority. Times do come when we must obey God rather than man, but they are usually rare exceptions. When a human authority requires us to do something that is forbidden by God, and restricts us from doing what God has called us to do, then we must obey God rather than man. The same applies when people try to exercise control over us when it exceeds the scope of their authority. A policeman can write us a ticket for breaking the traffic laws, but he cannot tell us what to believe or prevent us from going to church.

Living under a repressive political regime, a critical boss or abusive parents can be oppressive. But they cannot determine who we are unless we let them. There are times when it is legitimate and necessary to set up scriptural boundaries to protect ourselves from further abuse—for instance, a battered wife should report her abusive husband to authorities. We should righteously assert ourselves by setting boundaries and confronting any unbiblical behavior that is abusive.

It takes a great act of faith to trust God to work through less-than-perfect authority figures, but this is what He is asking us to do. In order to have a right relationship with God we need to be submissive to Him and to all governing authorities who are not violating biblical boundaries. Our commanding general, the Lord Jesus Christ, is saying, "Trust Me, be submissive to My authority and follow Me!" He will not lead us into temptation, but He will deliver us from evil (see Matt. 6:13).

Dana had been married for 12 years to Dave, and they had two children. She expressed feelings of emptiness, loneliness, tension, unhappiness and dissatisfaction in her marriage. Her husband, Dave, a committed Christian, had turned over every leaf to figure out how to help her with her discontentment. Nothing he could do seemed to make any difference. They had no financial worries, he was a devoted father, and he lavished her with compliments, vacations, flowers and attention. Despite this, she chose to fill the hollows in her life by partying with her girlfriends and dancing in bars with men she did not know for a "good time."

Dave confronted her with the temptation and perils this opened up for her, but she chose to ignore his call for caution. She subsequently chose to have an affair with a man at work; Dave was willing to forgive her when she confessed. Her acts of rebellion in the affair and in partying against his will strained the fabric of their relationship. Her family of origin had been unstable and void of intimacy. The rebellion in her current life, meant to fill the void, set her up to risk losing the security she had with her spouse.

Unfortunately, this story does not have a happy ending. She continued in a state of rebellion against God and her husband, and she resisted any further attempts at reconciliation. She needed to know who she was in Christ and that her need for acceptance, security and significance could only be realized as a child of the King. Instead, she rebelled against God's authority.

Pride Versus Humility

Pride often keeps us locked in a pattern of false thinking and prevents us from seeking the help we need. *I should be able to work this out myself!* That is tragic thinking, because we were never intended to live this life alone. God created Adam and Eve to live dependently upon Him. All temptation is an attempt to get us to live our lives independently of God. Pride is an independent spirit that wants to exalt self. "God opposes the proud, but gives grace to the humble" (Jas. 4:6). Pride says: "I can do this, I can get out of this myself." Oh, no, we can't! Such arrogant thinking sets us up for a fall: "Pride goes before destruction, a haughty spirit before a fall" (Prov. 16:18). Remember, we absolutely need God, and we necessarily need each other. Paul says, "Put no confidence in the flesh" (Phil. 3:3).

> ALL TEMPTATION IS AN ATTEMPT TO GET US TO LIVE OUR LIVES INDEPENDENTLY OF GOD.

Shame and self-deprecation are not humility. Humility is confidence properly placed. That is why we put no confidence in our flesh. Our confidence is in God. Self-sufficiency robs us of our sufficiency in Christ, because only in Christ can we do all things through Him who strengthens us (see Phil. 4:13). God intended for His children to live victoriously by having great confidence in Christ. "Not that we are competent in ourselves to claim anything for ourselves, but our competence comes from God. He has made us competent" (2 Cor. 3:5-6).

The following are some of the many ways that pride can reveal itself. Pride is

> having a stronger desire to do my will than God's will.
>
> being more dependent upon my own strength and resources than God's.
>
> believing too often that my ideas and opinions are better than those of others.
>
> being more concerned about controlling others than developing self-control.
>
> considering myself more important than others.
>
> having a tendency to think that I have no needs.
>
> finding it difficult to admit that I was wrong.
>
> having a tendency to be more of a people-pleaser than a God-pleaser.
>
> being overly concerned about getting the credit I deserve.
>
> being driven to obtain the recognition that comes from degrees, titles and positions.
>
> thinking I am more humble than others.

And pride is revealed in many other ways that God is convicting people of . . .

Consider the following example of how pride contributed to the destruction of a marriage. Mark's wife of 10 years was in an ongoing affair with her boss at work. Both Mark and his wife were Christians, and together they had four small children. They had married young and he had assumed a position of control and dominance in the relationship, giving her little room to experience herself as an individual. When her affair was disclosed, he became puffed up with his own righteousness and sexual purity. He began throwing Scripture verses at her, demanding she repent, grovel and submit to counseling to get straightened out. He was unwilling to look at his own controlling behavior that stymied intimacy. He refused to submit to church intervention when it was recommended that he go through the Steps to Freedom. He felt he was justified in throwing the first and subsequent stones, rather than examining his own heart for sin. He stopped further attempts at reconciliation and proceeded with a technically biblical divorce. Such self-righteous pride has kept many believers from being reconciled.

BONDAGE VERSUS FREEDOM

Habitual sin will cause conflicts in our relationships with others. Paul wrote, "Let us therefore lay aside the deeds of darkness and put on the armor of light. Let us behave properly as in the day, not in carousing and drunkenness, not in sexual promiscuity and sensuality, not in strife and jealousy. But put on the Lord Jesus Christ, and make no provision for the flesh in regard to its lusts" (Rom. 13:12-14, *NASB*). Repentance and faith in God are the only answers for breaking the bondage of sin, which so easily entangles us. We *can* be free from bondage to sin, because every believer is alive in Christ and is dead to sin (see Rom. 6:11).

People who have been caught in the sin-confess-sin-confess-sin-and-confess-again cycle may need to follow the instructions of James 5:16, "Confess your sins to each other and pray for each other so that you may be healed." Confession is not saying "I'm sorry"; it's saying "I did it." Those who have the ministry of reconciliation can offer the assurance of God's pardoning grace, for He promises that "If we confess our sins, he is faithful and just and will forgive us our sins and purify us from all unrighteousness" (1 John 1:9). Reconcilers can also lead needy believers to further genuine repentance.

This step is especially important for those who have been involved in sexual sin. Confession alone will not break the cycle of sexual sin: We also need to dedicate our bodies to righteousness. Paul says in Romans 6:11-13:

> In the same way, count yourselves dead to sin but alive to God in Christ Jesus. Therefore do not let sin reign in your mortal body so that you obey its evil desires. Do not offer the parts of your body to sin, as instruments of wickedness, but rather offer yourselves to God, as those who have been brought from death to life; and offer the parts of your body to him as instruments of righteousness.

It is our responsibility not to allow sin to reign in our bodies. Paul says that our bodies are temples of God, and if we sexually join ourselves with a prostitute we will become one flesh (see 1 Cor. 6:15-16). If we commit a sexual sin, we are using our bodies as instruments of wickedness, and sin will reign in our mortal bodies. If the sexual sin was with someone other than our married partner, we will bond together in the flesh. To break the power of that reign, we advise those who have sinned in this way to pray, asking their heavenly Father to reveal to their minds every sexual use of their bodies as an instrument of unrighteousness; and God does. As each incident comes to their mind, they renounce that use of their body and ask God to break that bond. They finish by prayerfully dedicating their bodies to God as instruments of righteousness, which we are urged to do by the mercies of God (see Rom. 12:1). This brings tremendous freedom for those who have been sexually promiscuous or sexually violated. For a more comprehensive explanation of this process, see Neil's book *A Way of Escape*.[4]

No one has to be convinced that sexual sins have caused incredible conflicts in homes and churches. Once the sin is exposed, reconciliation is possible if there is complete repentance by the one who is unfaithful, and if the one cheated on is willing to forgive. However, even when this happens, it still takes a long time for trust to be reestablished.

ACQUIESCENCE VERSUS RENUNCIATION

The last step in helping others find freedom in Christ is for them to renounce the sins of their ancestors and to actively take their place in Christ and resist the devil. The Ten Commandments reveal that the iniquities of fathers can be visited upon the third and fourth generation. This is evident in our society in the way abuse cycles are passed down from generation to generation. Jesus warned self-righteous Jews, "You testify against yourselves that you are the descendants of those who murdered the prophets" (Matt. 23:31). In other words: Like father, like son.

We are not guilty of our father's sins; but because they sinned, we will have to live with the consequences of their sin, and we will likely continue to live in the way we were taught by them unless we repent. Jesus said, "A pupil is not above his teacher; but everyone, after he has been fully trained, will be like his teacher" (Luke 6:40, *NASB*). Parents are the primary teachers in the first five years of our lives, and much of our personality and temperament has been established in those early and formative years.

When people repented in the Old Testament, they confessed their sins—and the sins of their fathers (see Lev. 26:39-40; Neh. 1:5-6; 9:2; Jer. 14:20; Dan. 9:10-11,16). We have the same responsibility today. "For you know that it was not with perishable things such as silver or gold that you were redeemed from the empty way of life handed down to you *from your forefathers,* but with the precious blood of Christ, a lamb without blemish or defect" (1 Pet. 1:18-19, emphasis added).

Expressing the closing prayer in the Steps to Freedom can produce some surprising results for the participants—results that are almost always related to their ancestors. One client had an apparition of what she thought was her father. After sharing what she saw, she said, "I'm responsible for my father." That, of course, is not true, but her Mormon background had led her to that belief. She found freedom after she renounced that lie and finished the Steps. Another lady experienced immediate spiritual opposition to renouncing the sins of her parents, who were deeply involved in Christian Science. One of my seminary students had to hold on to his chair to keep from running out of the room. His mother was a New Age psychic.

Helping Christians resolve their personal and spiritual conflicts is a ministry of reconciliation with God, and it has proven to be extremely beneficial for them. At the end of a conference on resolving personal and spiritual conflicts, people are given a chance to go through the Steps to Freedom in Christ in a group setting. Most people can process this on their own, since the Lord is the wonderful counselor; but some cannot. Therefore, a portion of our staff stay after a conference to provide personal appointments to those who cannot process the Steps on their own. We have given pretests and posttests three months later to those who have requested personal appointments. The following results from one church are indicative of the others:

Anxiety	59% improvement
Depression	57% improvement
Sense of worth	56% improvement
Anger	55% improvement
Negative habits	53% improvement

Tormenting thoughts	50% improvement
Fear	49% improvement
Sense of God's closeness	44% improvement
Bible reading and prayer	41% improvement
Health	38% improvement
Relationships	35% improvement

Obviously, with this kind of improvement in their lives, people are going to find it much easier to get along with others. One lady in full-time ministry said it this way, "My ability to process things has increased. Not only is my spirit more serene, my head is actually clearer! It's easier to make connections and integrate things now. It seems like everything is easier to understand now. My relationship with God has changed significantly."

CHAPTER 5

THE HEART OF RECONCILIATION

Matthew 18:21-35

Forgiveness is the fragrance the violet sheds
on the heel that has crushed it.
Mark Twain

I (Neil) was taking a break after giving a message on forgiveness, when a lady approached me. "Just forgive them? You want me to just forgive them for ruining my life!" she exclaimed. Ten years earlier her best friend had run off with her husband. From her perspective, they seemed to be getting on with their lives very well. They lived in a nice house and went on expensive vacations. Neither of them had shown any remorse for their sin, and neither had made any attempt to reconcile with her. Meanwhile this poor lady is reliving the pain every day and is hanging on to the past with all her might. For some sad reason, she thinks that hanging on to her bitterness is a way of getting even with them, when all it is really doing is contributing to her agony.

I said to her, "I see a hurting person with one arm thrust into the air with a closed fist, but the strong arm of God has a firm grasp around your wrist. You are not even hanging on to God, but He is hanging on to you. Your other arm is dragging you down while you firmly hang on to your past. Why don't you consider letting the past go and grab hold of God with all your might? All you are doing is hurting yourself."

"But you don't understand how badly they hurt me," she protested.

"They are still hurting you," I said. "Forgiveness is God's way of stopping the pain. When you let go of the past, it no longer has a hold on you and you reestablish communion with your heavenly Father who loves you."

She finally let go of the past—and the hurt. The next morning she was singing in the church choir, and the change in her countenance was noticed by everybody who knew her.

Forgiveness is the heart of reconciliation. Before we attempt to explain what forgiveness is and how to forgive, we need to make a clear distinction between the need to forgive others and the need to seek forgiveness from others. Jesus said, "If you are offering your gift at the altar and there remember that your brother has something against you, leave your gift there in front of the altar. First go and be reconciled to your brother; then come and offer your gift" (Matt. 5:23-24). In other words, if you have sinned against another person, do not carry on some religious piety, as though you have done nothing wrong, when the Holy Spirit is convicting you otherwise. Go to that person or persons with a repentant heart, ask for their forgiveness and offer to make reparations.

> **FORGIVING THOSE WHO HAVE WOUNDED US IS PRIMARILY AND INITIALLY AN ISSUE BETWEEN GOD AND OURSELVES.**

The initial course of action for those who need to forgive

others for their offenses is just the opposite. Do not go to the offending person; go to God. Forgiving those who have wounded us is primarily and initially an issue between God and ourselves. We cannot be right with God if we refuse to forgive others. This is made clear in the Lord's prayer: "Forgive us our debts, as we also have forgiven our debtors" (Matt. 6:12). Many people do not want to forgive another person because they wrongly believe that they have to go to them. In some cases, this would be impossible. The person they may need to forgive could be dead. In other cases, it would be unadvisable as it might set the person up for further abuse.

Some hold to the belief that we do not have to forgive unless the offender asks us to forgive, or at least acknowledges, the sin. The passage often cited to support this view is Luke 17:3-4: "If your brother sins, rebuke him, and if he repents, forgive him. If he sins against you seven times in a day, and seven times comes back to you and says, 'I repent,' forgive him." This passage does not say what to do if he does not ask for forgiveness. It does, however, teach us to continue forgiving even when offenders are not making much progress in overcoming their sinful habits. The disciples responded, "Increase our faith!" (v. 5), but their lack of faith was not their problem. Jesus explained that if they had faith the size of a mustard seed they could move mountains. The real question is: Did they—do we—really want to forgive such a person?

What if offenders never ask for our forgiveness? What if they have gone to their grave without ever admitting any wrong? Does that give us the right to remain in bitterness and refuse to forgive in defiance of God's instructions? With that kind of reasoning, any evil person could keep us in spiritual bondage for the rest of our lives, simply by remaining silent. Our relationship with God and our freedom in Christ cannot be dependent upon other people whom we have no right or ability to control.

Forgiving another person is primarily for the sake of *our* relationship with God—for the sake of healing our own soul. Forgiving others is not dependent upon the offender, but reconciliation is. So if we are able to forgive them from our hearts, reconciliation may follow—but only if the offenders assume their responsibility to be reconciled with God too.

THE NEED TO FORGIVE

The need to forgive others was taught by Jesus in Matthew 18:21-35 in response to Peter's question: "Lord, how often shall my brother sin against me and I forgive him? Up to seven times?" (v. 21, *NASB*). Jesus answered by saying that we should forgive another person "up to seventy times seven" (v. 22, *NASB*), but He was not suggesting that we keep a pocket calculator and tick off 490 times before we draw our gun. Forgiveness does not keep count. We continue forgiving as a part of our Christian lifestyle. To illustrate this, Jesus told a parable about a man who owed his master 10,000 talents. The debt was unpayable, since it was way beyond a lifetime wage. This is true of our moral debt with God. We could not pay it, so Jesus did.

Most offenses against us are unpayable. Suppose a person gossiped about you all over town and severely damaged your reputation. Then one day he or she came under conviction and asked you for forgiveness. You could sue for damages, but would that repay the debt? You could ask for public apology, but not all would hear it. Word may get around eventually, but you would have to live with the consequences of this sin for the rest of your life. Suppose that person never owned up to the slander, would you still need to forgive, and, if so, how?

To help us better understand this, Jesus continued His parable. The master ordered the slave and his family to be sold to pay off his debt. The indebted man had no choice but to beg for mercy. To make sense of this parable, we need to define three terms: "justice," "mercy" and "grace."

To mete out justice is to give people what they deserve. When Adam sinned, God had no choice but to give Adam what he deserved, which was spiritual death—the loss of eternal life. If we got what we deserved, we also would die in our sins, and all we would have to look forward to is hell—eternal separation from God.

God is also merciful. "Mercy" is not giving people what they deserve. In order to be merciful and yet preserve the justice of God, Jesus had to pay the price for our sin. The forgiveness of every debt is costly; the forgiveness of sin is a dear price indeed. Christ died to win forgiveness for us: He had to take the sins of the whole world upon Himself in order to forgive us; we have to take the sins of a few upon ourselves but seldom at the extreme price of our lives.

Grace is not the same as mercy. "Grace" is giving us what we do not deserve. Mercy does not go far enough. We are to be gracious and give people what they need: We must love one another.

In Jesus' parable, the slave was obviously grateful, but when a fellow slave owed him 100 denarii, he refused to forgive him. A denarii was a day's wages. We do not want to trivialize the offenses we have toward each other, but this parable makes it clear that the moral gap between God and ourselves is far greater than it is between the worst of us and the best of us. Consequently, the price that Jesus paid is far greater than what we will ever have to pay in order to forgive others. Since His forgiveness of us is the basis for our forgiveness of others, we need to realize the extent of the debt that we have been forgiven. Most people reading this book are probably good people, at least from a human perspective, but therein lies the danger. We can begin to think that our need for forgiveness is not very great, unlike other people who *really* need to be forgiven! We all equally need God's mercy and grace, and we must never forget it.

We should get up every morning and say, "Thank You, Lord,

for Your grace and mercy. I deserved eternal damnation, but You gave me eternal life. Out of deep gratitude for Your love, I am committing myself to be the person that You created me to be. Fill me with Your Holy Spirit and enable me to love, accept and forgive others in the same way You have loved, accepted and forgiven me." The slave in the parable did not do this. Instead, he ordered the man who owed him to be put in jail, which upset his fellow workers enough to report him to the master. As a result, "His lord, moved with anger, handed him over to the torturers until he should repay all that was owed him. So shall my heavenly Father also do to you, if each of you does not forgive his brother from your heart" (Matt. 18:34-35, *NASB*).

The imagery is that of torment for the purpose of teaching us something important. The root word for "torture" is also used in connection with the divine judgment spoken of in Revelation 9:5; 14:11 and 18:7. The verb form of the word "torture" is used by demons who begged Jesus not to torment them (see Mark 5:7; Luke 8:28). Those who refuse to forgive will experience spiritual torment of the mind. They cannot get the offender off their minds. Turning us over to the tormenters is not an act of revenge by God. He does not want us to live in the bondage of bitterness, so He disciplines us. He longs for us to forgive from our hearts and find the freedom of forgiveness.

WHAT FORGIVENESS IS NOT

In helping others work through the process of forgiveness, I have found it helpful to clarify what forgiveness is not.

Forgiveness Is Not Forgetting

God does not forget our sins, because He is an omniscient God. He could not forget even if He wanted to. When He says that He will not remember our sins, He is saying that He will not take our past offenses and use them against us in the future. He will remove them from us as far as the east is from the west. When we repeat the Lord's words in Communion, "Do this in remembrance of me" (Luke 22:19), we do not mean that we are to gather together occasionally and mentally recall what Jesus did for us over 2,000 years ago. It means that we should apply to our lives today what Jesus accomplished in His death and resurrection, because we are alive in Christ (see Rom. 6:1-11).

Forgetting a past offense may be a long-term by-product of forgiveness, but it is never a means to forgiveness. If you have ever tried to forget an atrocity committed against you, then you know what I mean. We cannot. I am not even sure the Lord wants us to forget such things. He wants us to forgive, from our hearts and to not bring the offenses up again. If spouses keep bringing up the past and using history against their mates, then they have not forgiven, and it will have a negative effect on their marriage. The same holds true for any relationship.

Forgiveness does not mean that we do not testify later for the purpose of seeking justice or for the purpose of confronting others when we carry out church discipline. What it does mean is that we forgive from our hearts in order to be right with God and to rid ourselves of bitterness. By doing so, we take the speck out of our own eyes, so we can see clearly. Only then can we properly approach an offending party for the sake of justice without bitterly seeking revenge. Offenders need to be brought to justice for their sake and for the sake of stopping the abuse, which brings up a second point.

Forgiveness Is Not Tolerating Sin

Jesus forgives, but He does not tolerate sin, and neither should we. A woman who was the director of a home for battered children and wives would come to speak to my seminary class. I was surprised to find out that local churches have not always been her closest allies. For one reason, some of the wives and children she had helped had come from the homes of "Christian leaders" in those churches. Another reason was the advice the victims had received from spiritual leaders in their churches: "Just go home, be submissive and trust God." The Bible does teach that women and children are to be submissive to their husbands and fathers, but that is not all the Bible teaches. It also teaches that there are governing authorities who have established laws to protect battered wives and abused children.

Suppose a man beat another woman in your church, a woman who was not his wife. Would you tolerate that? Never! But it's okay for a husband to beat his own wife? If a woman were abusing children in your church's nursery, would you tolerate that? But it's okay to abuse her own children simply because they are her children? Of course not! It is not only wrong, it is doubly wrong. God charges the husband to provide for and protect his wife and children, and the mother is to do likewise for her children. So when they become the abusers, the victims suffer double loss: Besides being victimized, they no longer have anyone to protect them. To illustrate this, suppose a woman comes to terms with the fact that her father sexually abused her. If she knows that her mother knew about it but did nothing to protect her, which one will be harder for her to forgive? It will be the mother.

We should report abusers to the governing authorities. Abusive people need help, and many will not seek it unless they are confronted and held responsible. We do not seek revenge, but we do seek justice. The shelter should teach victims to forgive their husbands and fathers, and then also teach them how to set up scriptural boundaries to stop further abuse. That is the only way to stop the cycle of abuse and to ensure that the abuser will no longer be allowed to harm others.

After my message on forgiveness, a wife and mother in tears

told me, "I know whom I need to forgive—my mother. But if I forgave her tonight, I know what will happen next Sunday. She will come over to our house and bad-mouth me all over again."

I said, "Why don't you put a stop to it?"

Surprised by my response, she asked, "Well, I'm supposed to honor my mother and my father, am I not?"

"How would it honor your mother to allow her to systematically destroy your marriage and family?" I asked.

While the Old Testament commandment to honor your parents is probably best understood as instruction for adult children to financially take care of their aging parents, that does not mean that younger children should not obey their parents. But this young mother was no longer under the authority of her parents who had given her away in marriage. Her primary responsibility now was to be a wife to her husband and a mother to her children. I suggested that she confront her mother about her abuse by saying something like this: "Mom, I want you to know that I love you and I am thankful for all that you have done for me, but I cannot put up with your verbal abuse anymore. It isn't doing you any good and it certainly isn't doing me any good. If you continue, I am going to insist that you stay away until you learn to respect my family and me. This cycle of abuse is going to stop right here. I have worked through my own bitterness and resentment, and I will not allow this problem to interfere with my responsibility to be a good wife and mother."

Forgiveness Is Not Stuffing Down Our Emotions or Denying Our Pain

If we are going to forgive from our hearts, then we have to do so from the core of our being. That means we have to acknowledge the hurt and the hate. Such denial is often the great evangelical slide-over—a generic forgiveness that doesn't identify the wrong being forgiven:

"Oh, I forgave my father."

"That's terrific, what did you forgive him for?"

"Things that he did to me."

"What did he do to you?"

"I don't want to talk about it!"

This person has not forgiven; he or she has tried unsuccessfully to forget it. Such people have tried to suppress past hurts, cover them up or deny that they happened, while God has been trying to surface it. If we try to bury our past, we do not bury it dead; we bury it alive, and it will surface in physical illnesses, emotional problems and interpersonal conflicts. We need to fully embrace the pain in order to let it go. If we forgive generically, we get generic freedom.

One young lady said, "I can't forgive my mother—I hate her!"

"On the contrary," I said, "now you can forgive her."

God is not asking us to deny our feelings. Such hypocrisy is inconsistent with the nature of God. We cannot be right with God and not be honest, and if necessary, God is going to have to make us real in order to be right with Him. Another way of saying this is, "Humble yourselves before the Lord, and he will lift you up" (Jas. 4:10). I have been with hundreds of people who have come to terms with their pain, and I have seen them experience the truth of Matthew 5:4: "Blessed are those who mourn, for they will be comforted." If they have truly forgiven their abusers, then they are free from them. Someone once said that to forgive is to set a captive free—only to realize that *you* were the captive. One lady explained, "That's why moving away from my mother didn't give me any mental peace. I was just running away from my responsibility, because I did not want to admit my bitterness and I did not want to confront my mother."

What Forgiveness Is

Concerning how we ought to live with one another, Paul wrote: "Get rid of all bitterness, rage and anger, brawling and slander, along with every form of malice. Be kind and compassionate to one another, forgiving each other, just as in Christ God forgave you" (Eph. 4:31-32). How has Christ forgiven us? He took our sins upon Himself. He bore the burden for the penalty of our sins. He voluntarily agreed to live with the consequences of our sins, which in His case meant death. Forgiveness is agreeing to live with the consequences of someone else's sin.

But That's Not Fair!
Of course it's not fair, but we will have to do it anyway. Everybody is living with the consequences of somebody else's sin. We are all living with the consequences of Adam's sin. The real choice is to live in the bondage of bitterness or in the freedom of forgiveness.

But Where Is the Justice?
It is in the cross of Jesus Christ our Lord and Savior. He died once for *all* our sins: my sins, his sins, her sins, our sins and their sins. Without the Cross, it is a moral offense to pardon the sins of others. "But," you will say, "I want justice." We will never have perfect justice in this lifetime. That is why we need to forgive others and to trust God that He will make it right in eternity. Everything will be made equitable after the final judgment. Christians should work for justice wherever they go, but justice will never be perfectly rendered in human courts.

But Why Should I Let Them Off My Hook?
That is precisely why you should forgive them: If you do not forgive, you are still hooked to them. The bondage of bitterness

keeps us chained to past offenders and abuses. However, if you let offenders off your hook, are they off God's hook? Not according to Romans 12:19-21:

> Do not take revenge, my friends, but leave room for God's wrath, for it is written: "It is mine to avenge; I will repay," says the Lord. On the contrary: "If your enemy is hungry, feed him; if he is thirsty, give him something to drink. In doing this, you will heap burning coals on his head." Do not be overcome by evil, but overcome evil with good.

God will mete out justice in His time—but usually that's later than we would like it. Our responsibility is to be like Christ and to live out the law of love as explained by Paul: "The entire law is summed up in a single command: 'Love your neighbor as yourself'" (Gal. 5:14). Living with the consequences of another person's sin does not mean that we fail to take a stand for the sake of righteousness, carry out church discipline or confront a brother who is sinning. It means that we do not let the sin of another person determine who we are or dictate how we are going to live. We have the choice whether we are going to sin in return for another's sin or love in return for that sin. In other words, we have a choice of living according to the flesh or living according to the Spirit. If we catch a person in sin, we should do as Paul instructed in Galatians 6:1-2: "Brothers, if someone is caught in a sin, you who are spiritual should restore him gently. But watch yourself, or you also may be tempted. Carry each other's burdens, and in this way you will fulfill the law of Christ."

The phrase "you who are spiritual" does not necessarily refer to spiritual maturity. It means we should respond in the power of the Holy Spirit as opposed to responding in the flesh. The flesh will respond in anger, seek revenge, demand immediate justice and defend itself. But if we live by the Spirit, we will not carry out the desires of the flesh (see Gal. 5:16). When we are filled with the Holy Spirit, we will gently restore the offender. The burden that we are asked to carry is the consequences of another's sin. That is the law of Christ as explained by Dietrich Bonhoeffer.

> The law of Christ, which it is our duty to fulfill, is the bearing of the cross. My brother's burden which I must bear is not only his outward lot, his natural characteristics and gifts, but quite literally his sin. And the only way to bear that sin is by forgiving it in the power of the cross of Christ in which I now share. Thus the call to follow Christ always means a call to share the work of forgiving men their sins. Forgiveness is the Christ-like suffering which it is the Christian's duty to bear.[1]

How to Forgive from the Heart

If possible, we should never pick up minor offenses in the first place. The imperfections of others and ourselves are something we all have to live with daily. We need to accept one another just as Christ has accepted us (see Rom. 15:7). We all have character flaws and bad moments that can irritate others. Forgiveness is the Christian lifestyle. We may not be consciously thinking it, but we can say by the way we live: "It is okay that you are not perfect, and I have no right to expect perfection from you. Therefore, I forgive you for not being fully sanctified." In that way we are modeling the unconditional love and acceptance of God.

However, some offenses cannot be overlooked. If we find ourselves being angry at another individual or offended by their behavior, then we need to decide whether we are going to forgive or not. Forgiveness is a crisis of the will. It is a decision not to seek revenge, not to live in resentment and not to wallow in bitterness. It is a decision to live with the consequences of the offender's sin and not to use it against them in the future. It is a decision to be like Christ and to maintain communion with Him.

We do not heal in order to forgive: We forgive in order to heal. The healing process cannot start, and reconciliation cannot take place, until we face the crisis of forgiveness. In the Steps to Freedom in Christ, we encourage people to pray and ask God to reveal to their minds whom they need to forgive. And God does, even in the face of denial. I have had people pray and then say, "Well, there is no one I need to forgive."

> WE DO NOT HEAL IN ORDER TO FORGIVE: WE FORGIVE IN ORDER TO HEAL.

To which I respond, "Would you just share the names that are coming to your mind right now?" Suddenly a page is filled with names. If God has commanded us to do something, then by His grace He will enable us to do it.

If the list is complete, we encourage them to pray: "Lord, I choose to forgive (name the person) for (what they did or failed to do), which made me feel (share the painful feeling)." The Lord not only provides the names, He also often brings up issues that have been buried in our subconscious. We encourage people to stay with every name until every issue has been faced whether it was a sin of commission or omission. For instance, "Lord, I forgive my father for verbally abusing me which made me feel worthless and unloved." By adding "how it made me feel" helps people get in touch with their emotions. It is very hard, if not impossible, to forgive from the heart if we do not get in touch with our core emotions.

After they have forgiven each person, we close by praying: "Lord, I choose not to hold on to my resentment. I thank You for setting me free from the bondage of my bitterness. I relinquish my right to seek revenge and ask You to heal my damaged emotions. I now ask You to bless those who have hurt me. In Jesus' name I pray, amen."

After you have forgiven from the heart, you will be tempted to pick up the offense again, because your memory has a tendency to replay your emotions. If you have successfully forgiven a person, you should be able to think about the person or see him or her without being emotionally overcome. That does not mean you like the person, but by the grace of God you can love them. If you catch yourself thinking about the past abuse or the person in a negative way, stop immediately what you are thinking, or you will find yourself emotionally embittered again. The decision to forgive is made every time you think about the abuse or see the person. To maintain your communion with God, you should develop a mental attitude that says, "Lord, I forgave that person, and I am not going to allow any thoughts in my mind to the contrary."

We cannot be dishonest about how we feel, and God is not asking us to do so. Forgiveness allows us to go to the other person with purer motives. If our purpose is not to restore them or be reconciled to them, then it is best we do not go.

Everybody faces the crisis of forgiveness. Let me share my first major encounter in ministry and what I learned from it. Having served as a campus pastor, youth pastor and associate pastor, this was my first role as a senior pastor. Within three months, I knew that I was headed for a power struggle, and I did not want it. I had always seen myself as a peacemaker, not a fighter, and I especially did not want to fight a member of my own church board. On the other hand, I was not easily intimidated and I was not afraid of confrontation. So I called Bob and asked if I could stop by his home. He agreed.

I told him that I did not feel good about our relationship and asked if I had done something to offend him. He assured me that I had not, but I knew nothing was resolved, so I asked if he would meet with me once a week to share any concerns that he had regarding me and my ministry. I encouraged him to be totally honest with me in private, rather than share any concerns that he had about my ministry at board meetings. I hated those weekly meetings, which were nothing but a verbal sparring match—and they went on for six months. I thought I could get along with anyone, but I learned the hard way that I could not have a meaningful relationship with another person if that person did not want to.

In the middle of that six-month ordeal, I requested permission from the church board to put together a tour to Israel and offered to use my vacation time. But Bob spoke up at the board meeting saying, "I know how these things work. If he can get enough people to go with him, he can go free, and that is like giving him a bonus." Not wanting to create any more tension on the board, I withdrew my request and used my vacation time to go with another group. I did not do that out of spite; I really wanted to go, and it turned out to be one of the greatest spiritual highs of my life. If nothing else, it was a respite from those Monday morning breakfasts!

As the tour guide led us through the Church of All Nations in the garden of Gethsemane, I knew why I was supposed to go. This beautiful mosaic structure enshrines the rock where they believe that Jesus prayed, "Father, if you are willing, take this cup from me; yet not my will, but yours be done" (Luke 22:42). I went back to that place of supreme resolution by myself the next day. I knew that I was in a special place for a special time in my life. This was where history's real battle had been fought and won. The mockery of a trial and the death march to the Cross would follow, but that was only the follow-through of the decision He had made in that garden.

In the throes of eternal agony, Jesus chose to take the sins of the world upon Himself. This went way beyond head knowledge for me. I sensed a renewing in my spirit of the purpose of the Cross and the message of forgiveness. I was rejoicing in my own renewal, but I also realized in a way I had never known before that I needed to forgive as I had been forgiven. Jesus had to take all the sins of the world on Himself. All He was asking me to do was to live with the consequences of one man's sin. I thought to myself, *I can do that. I will do that.*

I went home a different person, and the atmosphere of our first board meeting seemed to be much better. Not having me to pick on anymore, Bob went after my youth pastor. That did it! During the December board meeting, I took my stand. I told the board that they had to do something about Bob, or I was resigning. As far as I was concerned, our relationship was a sham, a disgrace to Christianity, and I was not going to have any part of it anymore.

The board met without us, and three weeks later I received a letter. "We have arranged a meeting for the two of you to ask each other for forgiveness, and then we can continue with our building plans." I was very disappointed. *Great,* I thought, *sweep it under the carpet and we can trip over it later!* I did go to the meeting, and I did ask Bob to forgive me for not loving him, because I did not. I was convicted about the feelings that I had for him, but I could not back down from my earlier stand. They had not dealt with the real issue, so I decided to resign.

Before I could resign, I got the flu. It was not the horrendous kind, but I felt like I should not subject the church to my illness. So our denominational leader spoke in my place and then joined us for dinner at our home. He was really pleased by the growth in our church. We had doubled in size and had plans to build new facilities at a new location, which God had given to us. Then I told him of my plans to resign. He was disappointed and disagreed with my decision, but my mind was made up.

I stayed home two days to make sure I was over the flu, and Wednesday morning I wrote out my resignation. By Wednesday evening my temperature was 103.5 and I had totally lost my voice. I have never been so sick before or since. It does not take a genius to recognize that God was not pleased with my decision. I did not resign that next Sunday—not because I was too sick, but because I still did not have a voice to speak.

When you are flat on your back there is nowhere to look but up. I was reading through the Gospel of Mark when I came to the following passage:

> They brought a blind man to [Jesus] and entreated Him to touch him. And taking the blind man by the hand, He brought him out of the village; and after spitting on his eyes, and laying His hands upon him, He asked him, "Do you see anything?" And he looked up and said, "I see men, for I am seeing them like trees, walking about." Then again He laid His hands upon his eyes; and he looked intently and was restored, and began to see everything clearly (8:22-25, *NASB*).

I got the message. I was seeing Bob like a tree. He was an obstacle in my path. He was blocking my goal. Oh, no, he wasn't! I was! In fact God used that man more than any other man on planet Earth to make me the pastor that God wanted me to be. The Lord has a way of putting obstacles in our path that we have no human way to deal with. We make plans in our own minds for the future. We think we know where we want to go and how we are going to get there. Then God comes along and plops a tree right in our path and says, "There, what are you going to do about that?" And our flesh is screaming, "Get me a chain saw!"

I cried out to God in my heart, "Lord, I don't love that man, but I know You do, and I want to. But there is nothing within me to love him except You, so You are going to have to touch me." He did! After two weeks of recovery, I was finally able to preach again. With a husky voice, I spoke on that passage in Mark. I told the congregation that there are three types of people in this world. First, there are those who are blind. Satan has blinded the minds of the unbelieving (see 2 Cor. 4:4). They need you and me to take their hands and lead them to Jesus. Second, there are those who see people like trees. We compare our leaves with one another and scratch each other with our branches. But we are not trees. We are children of God, created in His image. Third, there are those who see people clearly. God has touched them. I confessed to the congregation my own independent spirit and pledged my love to them. I gave an invitation that morning, and I do not even remember what I invited people to pray about. I was not prepared for what happened next.

People all over the auditorium came forward. There was not enough room in the front of the church to accommodate them, so the doors were opened and the people spilled out onto the lawn. The organist and pianist could no longer play because their tears blocked their vision. People were reaching across the aisles, asking each other to forgive them. I had not even talked about that! There could not have been any more than 15 people still seated. Would you care to guess who one of those 15 was? To my knowledge, the man never did change. Maybe he did not need to, but I did. I was never quite the same again. Nobody can explain what happened that morning apart from the grace of God.

I stayed at the church until our new buildings were completed; then God called me to teach at Talbot School of Theology. I wish I had known then how to preserve the fruit of that revival, but I did learn several lessons, which I pray I shall never forget.

First, the unconditional love, acceptance and forgiveness of God is the primary message of the Church. In writing to the church in Corinth, Paul said, "For I resolved to know nothing while I was with you except Jesus Christ and him crucified" (1 Cor. 2:2). True revival results in forgiveness, repentance and reconciliation.

Second, we cannot *preach* the good news and *be* the bad news. We are to love (see John 13:34), accept (see Rom. 15:7) and forgive (see Eph. 4:31-32), just as we have been loved, accepted and forgiven by God. In every way we are to be like Christ. We are living witnesses of the resurrected life of Christ within us. Our message is to repent from sin and to believe in God; our ministry is reconciliation. We are ambassadors for Christ (see 2 Cor. 5:18-20). May the grace of God enable us to represent Him well, and may He keep us from scandals that only bring shame to His name.

Third, God is fully capable of cleaning His own fish. It is not within our power to change anyone. God is the One who convicts us of sin. He alone can save us and set us free. Everything that happened in our church that morning can be credited to God alone. If I had had my way, I would have resigned, and I would probably be out of ministry to this day. I am so thankful that God struck me down. I pray that God would touch everyone. Neither hard work nor human ingenuity can pull it off. The one thing He wanted of me was brokenness—and even that He orchestrated. Only then could He work His grace through me: "'Not by might nor by power, but by my Spirit,' says the LORD Almighty" (Zech. 4:6).

CHAPTER 6

LOVING THE UNLOVELY

Luke 6:27-38

I am sure that most of us, looking back, would admit that whatever we have achieved in character we have achieved through conflict. It has come to us through powers hidden deep within us, so deep that we didn't know we had them, called into action by the challenge of opposition and frustration. The weights of life keep us going.

J. Wallace Hamilton

Have you ever wondered why the most difficult conflicts arise out of family, church or working relationships? We do spend most of our time in those relationships, but there are two deeper reasons why God works in our lives primarily through our committed relationships. First, in committed relationships we cannot consistently pretend to be someone that we are not. Our spouses, children, coworkers and Christian friends will see right through us, or at least discern that something is wrong. (Try having both a committed and hypocritical relationship with God at the same time and see what happens.)

Second, in committed relationships it is not easy to run away from our problems when they involve others. The Lord admonished us to stay committed to these relationships and to grow through the conflict. Paul wrote:

> We also exult in our tribulations, knowing that tribulation brings about perseverance; and perseverance, proven character; and proven character, hope; and hope does not disappoint, because the love of God has been poured out within our hearts through the Holy Spirit who was given to us (Rom. 5:3-5, *NASB*).

Rather than changing spouses, jobs or churches every time a conflict arises, we should stay committed and grow through it. There may be times when it is advisable to change churches or jobs but not if we are running away from conflicts that are intended to produce Christian character. If we do not learn to grow through the trials and tribulations of life, then we are doomed to face similar conflicts wherever we go.

Our hope does not lie in favorable circumstances, nor is it dependent upon other people. Our hope lies in our relationship with God and our growth in character. In the midst of interpersonal conflict, the only thing or person we have the power to change is ourselves. Living with imperfect people who are also in the process of conforming to God's image is inevitably going to result in conflict. From the wisdom literature of the Old Testament, we read, "Iron sharpens iron, so one man sharpens another" (Prov. 27:17, *NASB*). Have you ever stopped to think how iron sharpens iron? It generates a lot of heat, and sparks fly. Working through interpersonal conflicts is the refiner's fire where our character is forged.

Since conflict is inevitable, how have you learned to handle it? Do you withdraw or compromise? Yield to others or fight to win? Or do you try to manipulate other people and circumstances to your advantage? If you consider the value that you put on your relationships and your need to achieve, you can identify the following ways of dealing with conflict.

Conflict Styles

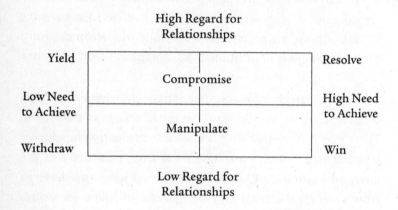

People with a high need to achieve and little regard for relationships are likely to approach conflict with the goal of winning. If they do not care about relationships or achievement, then they will probably approach conflict by trying to withdraw. On the other hand, manipulators have little or no regard for honest relationships and try to avoid personal confrontation. They work undercover and behind the scenes. Seeking middle ground is an attempt to compromise. Those who have a high regard for relationships will seek to resolve the conflict if they believe that something can be accomplished by it. If it is not worth the effort to seek resolution, they will probably yield to keep the peace.

There is no single right way to approach every conflict. Some situations call for compromise while others require us to fight for the sake of righteousness. Different temperaments and learning experiences affect how we approach conflict. Paul and Peter were both high achievers, and their natural inclination before their conversions was to win. Before they could become reconcilers, God had to literally strike Paul down (see Acts 9:1-9), and Peter was humbled more than once while he was with Christ (see Matt. 16:21-23; 26:69-75). Judas was a manipulator. Barnabas, the encourager, and John, the devotional one, would probably yield or compromise to keep the peace. "Compromise" is not a dirty word when it comes to living with others. It only becomes wrong when you compromise who you are as a child of God and what you believe to be true according to the Word of God.

Personal insecurity drives people to win, manipulate or run away. The basis for our sense of security is found in deep, meaningful relationships, and not necessarily in accomplishments. This becomes evident when insecure people do not win or get their way. The Bible does not say we always have to be right or win in every circumstance. It does, however, instruct us to be loving, kind, merciful, patient, forgiving, accepting and gentle. When the price for winning costs us a meaningful relationship, the price is probably too high. On the other hand, yielding or compromising to keep the peace when something could have been resolved will also be costly in the long run. We can sweep something under the carpet for a time, but eventually we will trip over it. The ultimate goal is to resolve our conflicts, not just manage them.

How we deal with conflict is largely related to what we have learned from our parents and teachers. What they modeled was more caught than taught, and you have probably adopted your primary response to conflict from one of these influencers. As you think about the preceding chart and how you handle conflict, consider the following questions:

1. Which conflict style typified your father, and how has that affected you?
2. Which conflict style typified your mother, and how

has that affected you?

3. Which conflict style typifies you?
4. Which parent are you most like?
5. How well did, or do, you relate to this parent as opposed to the other parent?
6. Which conflict style best typifies your spouse? The person you are in conflict with?

People have different experiences, interests, concerns and perspectives when it comes to resolving conflicts. The best opportunity to resolve the conflict will emerge when every person's perspective is heard and appreciated. By entertaining diverse ideas and perspectives, you have the potential to unearth more alternatives for resolution. Not handled correctly, conflicts can damage relationships and lead to stalemates rather than to decisions. Deciding whether facing a conflict will be constructive or destructive can be determined by considering the following ideas.

Destructive when:	Constructive when:
People do not understand the value of conflict that naturally comes when other opinions and perspectives are shared.	People understand the need to hear the other side so that responsible decisions can be made.
A competitive climate implies a win-lose situation.	A cooperative spirit implies a commitment to search for a win-win solution.
"Getting my own way" is all-important.	Doing it God's way is all-important.
People reflexively employ defense mechanisms including: denial, suppression, blame, withdrawal and aggression.	People assume that disagreements evolve from another person's sincere concern for truth.

People are locked into their own viewpoints, unwilling to consider the perspectives and ideas of others.	People believe that they will eventually come to an agreement that is better than any one individual's initial suggestion.
People resort to personal attacks instead of focusing on the issues.	Disagreements are confined to issues rather than personalities.
Personal ideas and opinions are valued over relationships.	Relationships are more important than the need to win or be right.

In destructive relationships, cliques form, subgrouping takes place, deadlocks occur, stalemates are common, and tension remains high. People in these settings live with a lot of unresolved personal conflicts. These issues would have to be resolved before reconciliation is possible. When conflict resolution is constructive, there is unity and a high level of trust. Sharing is open and honest.

When people attempt to resolve interpersonal conflicts, they do not have to perfectly agree with each other. Giving all parties an equal opportunity to express their views and share their feelings while working toward a resolution is what is important. The person in the position of authority will be responsible for the final decision regardless of who makes it. It is a wise leader who makes a decision only after hearing all the facts and humbling oneself before God. If confronted with choosing between the path of pride or humility, choose humility. You will lose no one's respect by saying, "You were right and I was wrong."

The three criteria for successful conflict resolution are: a righteous relationship with God, love for each other and the ability to communicate. We will look at possible styles of communication as they relate to our regard for relationships and achievement:

COMMUNICATION STYLES

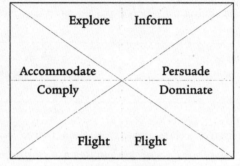

People with a high need to achieve tend to control the conversation. If they have some regard for relationships, they will try to persuade the other person. If they do not care for others or value relationships, they tend to dominate. Controllers assume the primary role in discussion, and the conversation is usually one-way. On the other extreme, people who have a low need to achieve tend to relinquish control of the conversation to other parties. They accommodate and comply. They are usually quite receptive to others, but they prefer a passive role and shift the responsibility for conversation to others.

People who have little regard for relationships tend to withdraw. They will fight if they want to achieve something and flee if they do not. They avoid intimate relationships. They block communication by neither soliciting nor contributing to the conversation. On the other extreme, people who have a high regard for relationships seek to develop the relationship by adapting to the styles of informing and exploring. These styles involve mutual sharing among equals. Communication is two-way. Both attempt to contribute to the conversation and seek to understand each other.

How did we learn to communicate? The same way we learned to deal with conflict. Our primary teachers have been our parents and significant others. Consider the same questions you looked at earlier, but this time in reference to communication:

1. Which communication style typified your father, and how has that affected you?
2. Which communication style typified your mother, and how has that affected you?
3. Which communication style typifies you?
4. Which parent are you most like?
5. How well did, or do, you relate to this parent as opposed to the other parent?
6. Which communication style best typifies your spouse? The person you are in conflict with?

In order to relate to one another from a Christian perspective, we have two primary responsibilities. First, we are responsible for our own character. Again, let me repeat, God's will for our lives is our sanctification (see 1 Thess. 4:3). There is no plan B for our lives. In order to accomplish this goal, God may have to torpedo some of our plans—even disrupt our career goals if that is what it is going to take. No biblical principles help us decide whether we should be carpenters, plumbers or engineers. But the Bible gives us a lot of instructions concerning what *kind* of carpenters, plumbers and engineers we are supposed to be. If we desire to be reconciled to others, we must choose the path of godly character. From God's perspective it is always *character before career, maturity before ministry* and *being before doing.*

Paul asks: "Who are you to judge someone else's servant? To his own master he stands or falls. And he will stand, for the Lord is able to make him stand" (Rom. 14:4). It may be appropriate to judge ourselves but not others. Yet we are instructed to discipline one another. What is the difference? Judgment is related to character, while discipline is related to conduct. Discipline is not punishment, which is a law concept. Punishment is an eye for an eye, and it is always retroactive. God does not punish us when we do something wrong, He disciplines us, so we do not do it again. Discipline superintends future choices. "God disciplines us for our good, that we may share in his holiness. No discipline seems pleasant at the time, but painful. Later on, however, it produces a harvest of righteousness and peace for those who have been trained by it" (Heb. 12:10-11). So if we have to confront someone for the purpose of discipline and reconciliation, it must be based on the person's conduct, not character.

If we are to relate to one another from a Christian perspective, our second primary responsibility is to love one another—to meet one another's needs. What would life be like if all believers assumed responsibility for their own characters and were committed to loving their neighbors as themselves? That may not be fully realized until we get to heaven, but surely we can and must begin living that way now. The character of love and the commitment to love one another is the core of our sanctifying process. Paul admonishes Timothy to avoid discussions that lead to controversies "rather than God's work—which is by faith. The goal of this command is love, which comes from a pure heart and a good conscience and a sincere faith" (1 Tim. 1:4-5).

When people are caught in conflict with one another, they often abdicate the responsibility to love and do the opposite. They begin questioning or criticizing the character of others while looking out for their own needs. There is no way that we can be reconciled if we relate to each other in that way. We have abdicated our biblical responsibilities when we no longer want what is best for the other person. Both our character and our orientation toward one another are wrapped up in one word, "love," or *agape*.

To understand God's love, it is helpful to know that the Greek word "agape" is used in Scripture both as a noun and as a verb. When used as a noun, love is the highest of character attainment.

God is love (1 John 4:16).

Love is patient, love is kind. It does not envy, it does not boast, it is not proud. It is not rude, it is not self-seeking, it is not easily angered, it keeps no record of wrongs. Love does not delight in evil but rejoices with the truth. It always protects, always trusts, always hopes, always perseveres (1 Cor. 13:4-7).

We should be able to say every year, "I am more loving than I was last year. People are responding more to my kindness, gentleness and patience. I have a greater degree of self-control, and I am experiencing more joy and peace with myself and others." If the fruit of the Spirit is not becoming more evident in our lives, then we are not growing.

The love of God is unconditional, because it is not dependent upon the object of His love. God loves us, not because we are lovable, but because God is love. It is His nature to love us. It would go against God's nature to not love us. That is the major difference between agape and *phileo*, another Greek word meaning "brotherly love." This brotherly love describes the common interests of a friendship (see Jas. 4:4) or even the affection of the false kiss which Judas used to identify Jesus at His arrest (see

Matt. 26:48; Mark 14:44; Luke 22:47-48). In order to love the unlovely, we must take on the character of God, and every believer can express God's character because we participate in His divine nature when our souls are in union with God (see 2 Pet. 1:4). We become more and more capable of loving others when we become more and more like Christ.

Jesus said, "A new command I give you: Love one another" (John 13:34). It was a new command, because apart from Christ, we could not be commanded to do something we were humanly incapable of doing. He is commanding us to love, not like, one another. Even with the grace of God within us, we cannot pretend to like mean-spirited people who are doing evil things to us. We can, however, do the loving thing by the grace of God. This is where the ministry of reconciliation gets tough. Jesus said, "But I say to you who hear, love your enemies, do good to those who hate you, bless those who curse you, pray for those who mistreat you" (Luke 6:27-28, *NASB*).

How do we love those who hate us? We do good deeds on their behalf. The word "hate" here is referring more to a bad attitude or emotional disposition. Jesus is talking about those who are not inclined to like us. They are not necessarily treating us badly; they simply do not like us. The Lord is saying that we should respond to their bad attitude by doing good deeds. Actions speak louder than words. These people are the neighbors we are commanded to love as ourselves.

While working as an engineer, I had a coworker who liked to make fun of Christians. Hardly a staff meeting went by where he did not make fun of my faith. Loving him became a personal challenge. One day he suffered a personal tragedy that could not be remedied by any natural means. To my surprise, he stopped by my cubicle and asked me if there were people in my church who prayed for others. His attitude toward me and other Christians became more positive.

The next test of love is to bless those who curse us. Now the challenging objects of our love are saying things about us that are not good. How are we to respond? Doing the loving thing may not work. In fact, they may resent it. So we are to bless them. The Greek word for "bless" is *eulogeo*. "Eulogeo" literally means "to speak well of." To speak well of, or bless, those who curse us requires the grace of God, because our flesh would like to point out their faults and defend ourselves. We are most like Christ when we are not defensive in the face of slander. "When they hurled their insults at him, he did not retaliate; when he suffered, he made no threats. Instead, he entrusted himself to him who judges justly" (1 Pet. 2:23). We do not have to draw upon our old defense mechanisms now that we are alive in Christ. Christ is our defense, and we do not need any other. Defending ourselves will only bring more verbal assault.

I have always found it helpful to know that nobody bothers to tear down another person out of a position of strength. Mature Christians do not do that. Those who are critical of others are hurt people, and if we keep that in mind, it is a little easier to take their verbal abuse. Out of their pain and failure, they lash out at others. Maybe they think they can pull us down to their level, but we cannot be tempted to go there. I grew up with the folk proverb: If you can't say anything nice about the other person, then don't say anything at all. So if we cannot bless them—say something good about them—then we say nothing at all and trust God to be our defense. Is that easy? No, it is hard, but it is a lot easier than to get into a verbal battle where you both lose and the path of reconciliation gets harder.

The third test of our character is to love those who are mistreating us. Neither good deeds nor good words will probably work in this case. So we are instructed to pray for them (see Luke 6:28). Jesus is not suggesting that we pray for their demise, but rather for their victory over sin. Ask God to give them new life in

Christ and to meet their deepest needs. Their souls are in anguish, and they need to experience the grace of God just as we have.

The Lord's applications for the above instructions do not get any easier. "If someone strikes you on one cheek, turn to him the other also. If someone takes your cloak, do not stop him from taking your tunic. Give to everyone who asks you, and if anyone takes what belongs to you, do not demand it back" (Luke 6:29-31). It is better to suffer physical abuse and to lose material possessions than to let our hearts be corrupted. However, the Lord is not emphasizing passivity in the face of evil in this passage. The emphasis is on the concern that we should have for others. Refraining from doing evil often meant suffering from evil as our Lord modeled (see 1 Pet. 2:20-24), when He prayed for His enemies (see Luke 23:34) and died for them (see Rom. 5:8). If someone strikes us on our cheek, we are not to reciprocate in kind, which can only make matters worse. Returning evil for evil will not accomplish anything other than to add to the pain.

On the other hand, if someone broke into my house and threatened my family, I would do all within my power to stop him or her from doing something we would all later regret. If the opportunity lends itself, I would sit down with the person and ask what motivated him to take such drastic measures. If he were desperately in need, by the grace of God I would give him something to alleviate his suffering, whether it were food or clothing. It is better to suffer double loss (a cloak and a tunic) than to respond in the flesh. We cannot let desperate people determine who we are. Their desperate acts indicate how badly they are hurting, and we have to see beyond that and respond in such a way as to meet their needs. When we love those who appear to have no regard for us, we are behaving according to our true identity in Christ. "Then your reward will be great, and you will be sons of the Most High, because he is kind to the ungrateful and wicked" (Luke 6:35).

All the instruction given above can be summed up in the golden rule: "Do to others as you would have them do to you" (Luke 6:31). This is the law of grace, as opposed to the law of retaliation. The following negative form of the golden rule was written by the Hebrew scholar, Hillel, and it was well-known at the time of Christ. "What is hateful to you, do not to your neighbor: that is the whole Torah, while the rest is the commentary thereof" (Shabbath 31a). In other words, do not do anything hateful to your neighbor. But the Lord put it in the positive. We should do to others what we would like them to do to us and do it whether they reciprocate or not. "Jesus himself said: 'It is more blessed to give than to receive'" (Acts 20:35).

When I was pastoring, an old man thanked me for my message and then handed me a note on his way out of the church. It read, "It is one of life's greatest compensations that you cannot sincerely help another without helping yourself in the process." He was right. Jesus said, "Give, and it will be given to you. A good measure, pressed down, shaken together and running over, will be poured into your lap. For with the measure you use, it will be measured to you" (Luke 6:38). Being an old farm boy, I know exactly what He means. If you owe someone a bushel of oats, you can fill the bushel basket carefully and scrape it off with a two by four. That is a fair measure. Or you can shake the bushel basket while it is being filled so that it settles—and then keep filling it up until it runs over. That is better than a fair measure.

I learned a similar principle when I was in the Navy. I could do enough to keep the brass off my back, and say with my fellow sailors, "Close enough for government work." I did my fair share and just enough to get by. But that was not very satisfying, nor was it rewarding. So I adopted a new philosophy, which could be stated like this: Whatever life asks of you, give just a little bit more. I have tried to live that way ever since. If my job started at 9:00 A.M., I was there at least 15 minutes early, and I usually left

15 minutes after closing time. I did not realize at the time how biblical that was. We get out of life what we put into it. If we want a friend, we should be a friend. If we want someone to love us, we should love the other person. It is not enough to stop treating people negatively. We should treat them in the same way we want to be treated whether they do or not.

Will others always reciprocate in kind? No! And the hope that they will reciprocate cannot be our motivation. The grace of God within us will compel us to give to others in need without any hint of repayment. As our character develops, it will become our nature to give to those who are needy. When Jesus was invited for dinner, he said to the host,

> When you give a luncheon or dinner, do not invite your friends, your brothers or relatives, or your rich neighbors; if you do, they may invite you back and so you will be repaid. But when you give a banquet, invite the poor, the crippled, the lame, the blind, and you will be blessed. Although they cannot repay you, you will be repaid at the resurrection of the righteous (Luke 14:12-14).

Reconciliation with others is not a mechanical process that we go through based on biblical rules and regulations. It is a lifestyle of character transformation. As we become more and more like Christ, we will learn to be merciful as our heavenly Father is merciful (see Luke 6:36). We will learn to suspend our judgment of others, and then we will not be condemned; we will learn to forgive and experience even more the forgiveness of others (see v. 37). We do not do this to manipulate other people or the circumstances of life. We do it because it is what Jesus would do.

I was in Bogota, Columbia, when I heard on CNN that Princess Diana had died. Within a week, Mother Teresa also died. They were the two most well-known women at the end of the twentieth century, and you could not find two people more different. One was very rich; the other had taken a vow of poverty. One was very pretty; the other was not physically attractive. They did, however, have something in common. Both were royalty, one in a physical kingdom and the other in His kingdom. Both were afforded a state funeral even though protocol did not require it for either one. We could debate the morality of the one and the theology of the other, and totally miss the point. The whole world honored these two women for the same reason: We perceived that they cared.

Love for God and one another is the greatest apologetic for our faith, and the one essential prerequisite for a ministry of reconciliation. People do not care how much we know, until they know how much we care. Any attempt to be reconciled with others must be motivated by love. They have to sense that we have their best interest at heart. There cannot be any ulterior motive, or they will see right through us—and God cannot bless such a ministry. Jesus said, "But go and learn what this means: 'I desire mercy, not sacrifice.' For I have not come to call the righteous, but sinners" (Matt. 9:13).

This truth was powerfully illustrated by the testimony of a pastor and his wife. As we were having lunch one day, she shared how the Lord was calling her to work in the only ministry in Portland, Oregon, that was trying to help those struggling with homosexuality. The problem was that it was a closed group. In other words, to attend you had to be one of them. Realizing that, she became very self-conscious about her slacks and her hair, which was cut quite short. She thought to herself, *Maybe I'd better let my hair grow out and wear a dress, or they will think I am one of them!* Then the Lord spoke to her, "My dear daughter, that is what I did!"

Jesus never said, "Let's get one thing straight. I am not one of you. I am God!" On the contrary, He took on the form of a man and fully identified with us, but He did not identify with our sin. This pastor's wife decided to sit with these people and identify with them but not their sin. Within a few months, she became their spokesperson and her husband became the chairman of their board. They are carrying on their ministry of reconciliation and setting captives free. We cannot *preach* the good news and *be* the bad news. Jesus said, "By this all men will know that you are my disciples, if you love one another" (John 13:35).

HOW PEACEMAKERS LIVE

We are therefore Christ's ambassadors, as though God were making his appeal through us. We implore you on Christ's behalf: Be reconciled to God.

2 CORINTHIANS 5:20

PART II

CHAPTER 7

UNDERSTANDING CONFLICT

To prefer my own happiness to my neighbor's was like think-
ing that the nearest telegraph post was really the largest.

C. S. Lewis, *Surprised by Joy*

Selfish desires, injustice, discrimination, oppression and the desire for power fuel fights, quarrels and war. No one is exempt from conflict as long as we live in this broken and sinful world. It comes to every person, family, organization, business, church, community and nation. Conflict is as universal as sin.

Some stories of conflict make us cry. Who does not shudder when hearing about the Holocaust in Germany, the Killing Fields in Cambodia or the Genocide in Rwanda? The inhumane deprivation, torture and murder make us cringe. How deep is this sin in the human heart, anyway? What turned "good people" into ruthless and sadistic dehumanizers, tormenters, killers? To our shock, we learn that the people who did such things were not much different from us. Most of these perpetrators justified themselves as following orders in military action or as acting in self-defense.

In their insightful book, *Unlocking Horns: Forgiveness and Reconciliation in Burundi,* Chuck's good friends and colleagues David Niyonzima and Lon Fendall tell of experiencing terrifying conflict at its worst.[1] The two major tribes of the countries of Burundi and Rwanda, the Hutus and Tutsis, belong to the same race, speak the same language, share a common history, live in integrated villages and towns and sometimes intermarry. David, for example, is Hutu, and his wife, Felicity, is Tutsi.

On October 25, 1993, David's class at the Kwibuka Pastoral Training Center was in session when he heard gunfire from a town two miles away. Not unusual. Soldiers exerted lethal force every once in awhile. Things were especially tense at this time because four days earlier the Hutu president, Melchior Ndadaye, had died because of an assassin's bullets.

In quiet Kwibuka, life went on as normal. David enjoyed teaching and liked his students, who were mainly Hutus but also included three Tutsis. They had just taken a break from class and were enjoying the sunshine outside when they saw a group of soldiers and civilians approaching from a distance. Seconds later, without warning or making any demands, the soldiers started shooting their automatic weapons.

Everyone scattered, fear pumping adrenaline through their bodies and brains. David ran a few hundred yards to an old auto mechanic's shed, unused since the 1980s. Years before, missionaries had dug a grease pit in the shed for changing oil and doing other work on their vehicles. An old car was over the open pit at the moment. David slipped inside the shed, locked the door and hid in the grease pit. Outside, the rifles exploded with unbelievably loud noise, gunning down students and anyone else in their range. They were hunting for Hutus but mistakenly killed two of the three Tutsi students as well.

David heard soldiers' voices outside the shed where he was hiding. Then they kicked down the door and looked around. Deciding no one was inside, they left. In time, the shooting stopped. David waited an hour, two hours, three hours—all day and all night. As a well-known Hutu, he assumed the soldiers would keep looking for him. The next morning, wanting to appear inconspicuous, he put on a pair of mechanic's overalls and quickly walked to the home of his parents. Knowing the danger of the situation and having lost another son to similar violence 20 years earlier, his parents quickly hid him in the attic. In the meantime, his wife, Felicity, and son, James, showed up safe and sound! They wept, hugged, laughed and cried some more.

After a week of hiding out, the Lord's voice came clearly, challenging David just as He had challenged Elijah in the cave, in 1 Kings 19:9: "What are you doing here?" With a mixture of dread and relief, David emerged from his hiding place and went back to the site of the murders at Kwibuka. Over the next few days, he and a few friends buried 25 bodies, some of them were students and some civilians who had been fleeing nearby Gitega before they died of their gunshot wounds.

For David, a time of anger, depression and questioning God followed. "Why" questions flooded his mind: *Why did so many have to die, especially the students who had so much potential in God's work? Why had there been no warning that something like this might happen? Why hadn't God told us to flee? What had we done to make the informants bring the soldiers to our school? Why, God, why?* Grief, horror, anger, fear and frustration raged within.

But there also came an inner urge to apply literally Jesus' teaching about loving and forgiving enemies. David had recognized one of the informants who had led the soldiers to the Bible school. From the Holy Spirit, he felt two directives: He should not press any legal charges, and he should go to the conspirators and tell them they were forgiven.

An inner debate raged within him about whether this idea was sane or crazy. In town, David unexpectedly encountered Filbert, the very man he had recognized on the day of the killings. To his own surprise, David found himself saying to

Filbert, "By God's power, I forgive you for your part in bringing the soldiers to kill our students at Kwibuka."

Filbert looked as if someone had hit him between the eyes. "What are you saying? You're badly mistaken. I was not involved at all in the incident." He lied!

"I'm not here to argue with you, Filbert. I'm telling you that I know you were one of those in the group. But I'm not accusing you either. I'm forgiving you. Jesus has asked me to forgive those who have wronged me, and by His power I'm doing exactly that." David's words hit home. Filbert was overwhelmed and speechless, although it did not bring him to confess.

In David Niyonzima's own words:

I, in turn, was overwhelmed with joy and relief. I felt that a heavy load had been lifted from my back. I felt released. Peace spread through my body and spirit. Fear and anger gave way to boldness and love. It was like Saul in Damascus, when Ananias had prayed for him. Scales fell from Saul's eyes. He arose, was baptized, took food and regained his strength. Scales fell from my eyes as well. I had only been able to see the evil in others, but my new eyes permitted me to see a person whom God loved and was willing to forgive. How could I not forgive someone who was freely being offered God's grace and forgiveness?

A simple handshake followed, but the act of forgiving turned David from having a spirit of revenge to a spirit of reconciliation. With boldness from the Lord, he began to travel, speak and address people through the radio to come out of hiding. God continued to expand David's ministry, and today he is the leader (legal representative) of the evangelical Friends denomination in Burundi. From that day onward, he has used his influence as a peacemaker.[2]

Conflicts are here to stay. The shooting at Columbine High School and the September 11 terrorist attacks are grim reminders of severe crises in the United States. In other countries, hostilities go on for generations or even centuries. Think of Kosovo or the Middle East. Not all conflicts, however, are on the national and international level. For most of us, they are on a much more personal level, and they keep showing up at the most inconvenient times. They arise at work, surface in marriage and even disrupt harmony in our churches.

WHAT IS CONFLICT?

Conflict begins when people disagree, often sharply. It emerges when people want their own way and believe it is the right way. It becomes intense when people choose sides (always the right side, of course), justify themselves and blame others. As the tension builds, it will either find resolution or turn into a collision, or even an explosion.

"Conflict" usually refers to a hostile encounter, a collision of divergent ideas, interests or persons. Synonyms include "disagreement," "clash," "divergence," "argument," "quarrel," "discord."

CONFLICT IS THE COLLISION OF DIFFERING DESIRES.

Attorney Ken Sande, in his helpful and biblical book *The Peacemaker*, defines conflict as "a difference in opinion or purpose that frustrates someone's goals or desires."[3] Conflict comes from differences—with tension. In fact, it might be simply defined as, "Conflict equals differences plus tension."[4]

Our working definition will be rather simple: Conflict is the collision of differing desires.

WHAT CAUSES CONFLICT?

The reasons for conflict are many; some are good and some are bad. People vary in likes and dislikes. That's good. People want their own way. That's bad. People disagree. That's understandable. People want to win and force others to lose. That's bad. People hold competing loyalties, fight over limited resources and want power to bring about change. That could start good and end up bad.

As long as we have people, we will have differences. As long as we have differing desires, we will have tension. As long as we have tension, we will have collisions. Whenever we have collisions of differing beliefs and values, we have conflict.

People create problems, and problems have a process, a history. Every conflict includes people, problems and process, and any of the three may lie at the root. Every peacemaker who wants to bring about reconciliation would be wise to become aware of not only the problem, but the people who caused it and the process that got them into a conflict in the first place.

THE ROOT OF CONFLICT

At its heart, conflict is a spiritual problem. James, the brother of our Lord, goes to the heart of the issue: "What causes fights and quarrels among you? Don't they come from your desires that battle within you? You want something but don't get it. You kill and covet, but you cannot have what you want. You quarrel and fight" (Jas. 4:1-2).

Name an evil desire—greed, hatred, jealousy, rage, etc.—any can lead to conflict. Why? Because of our fallen nature. At our core we are self-centered and deceitful. And because we are deceived, we are blind and self-justifying.

When we are tempted, we know it. When we are accused or are accusing others, we know it. But when we are deceived, we do *not* know it. Because as soon as we know we are deceived, our eyes are opened to the evil and we are not deceived anymore. So what are we to do? How can we put ourselves at the right starting point to deal with the spiritual root of conflict? We begin by getting our eyes off ourselves and on the Lord Jesus Christ. This same principle applies in every situation (see Col. 3:1-2; Heb. 12:2). We must step back and consider our motives. Why do we *really* want whatever object we're desiring? Is it to please and glorify God? Or is it to satisfy our own sinful lusts?

> **TO BEGIN TO DEAL WITH THE SPIRITUAL ROOT OF CONFLICT, PRAY THIS SIMPLE PRAYER, "LORD, OPEN MY EYES TO MY FALSE DESIRES AND SELFISH LONGINGS."**

The moment of truth hits when we actually realize and acknowledge, "Even if I get everything I desire, all I have belongs to God. He may not want me to have it." After we lift our eyes to Christ, we need the people of God to help us take our blinders off (see Heb. 3:12-13). We need to be involved in church, in Bible study, in Sunday School, in an accountability group, in a recovery group. We need other people, using their spiritual gifts and insights, to open our eyes to how we have lost perspective in conflict.

To begin to deal with the spiritual root of conflict, pray this simple prayer, "Lord, open my eyes to my false desires and selfish longings." Then listen to the Word of God when it is preached or taught. Hear the criticism of a spouse or adolescents or friends or anyone who holds you accountable. Ask, "The last time I got what I wanted, did I use it for God's glory?" If not, why should He give it to me this time? Beware of what you covet. The love of that money—or prestige, power, etc.—is a root of all kinds of evil (see 1 Tim. 6:10).

SOURCES OF CONFLICT

Conflict can come from any number of sources. David Cimbora, Ph.D., who teaches at the Rosemead School of Psychology at Biola University in La Mirada, California, suggests the following three: role differences, value differences and perception differences.

Role Differences

Tensions can arise because of the differing desires that occur in the various relationship roles we experience—government/citizen, husband/wife, boyfriend/girlfriend, boss/employee, parent/child, landlord/renter, seller/buyer, professor/student. Anyone who has lived on both sides of these relationship roles will understand the built-in differences in desires and goals. Each role wants different things, expects different things, needs different things. When the other person in the relationship role does not meet our expectations, undermines our goals or causes us stress, then tension begins to build. Over time, our differing desires collide, and we have conflict. Most of us are not surprised by this. It is so common that we expect reasonable conflict between these roles and often work hard to resolve the conflicts as quickly and amicably as possible.

Value Differences

It is also no surprise that people differ in their values. Think of the various worldviews, belief systems, philosophies, religions, ideologies, political systems and moral beliefs among people. We do not expect Democrats and Republicans to agree; we expect conflict. We know that Islam, with its laws against converting to another religion, will conflict with Christianity, with its message about personal faith in Jesus Christ. Value differences will often bring people into conflict because, at times, their goals, pathways and desires will collide.

Value differences can collide within ourselves as well, causing us tension and stress. Our conflicting inner values can spill over into our relationships too. Consider some examples of quality of work versus making more money:

- Shall I see more patients per hour, making more money, or fewer patients per hour, making less money but giving better care?
- Shall I build the house with meticulous workmanship and the best quality materials, even if I make less profit, or shall I ignore mistakes that don't show and use cheaper materials?
- Shall I work diligently all day long at my hourly rate or relax, enjoy my fellow employees and waste a little time for the same pay?

Making these choices will most likely affect our relationships with others, and making an unrighteous choice will bring about conflict.

Perception Differences

One of the surprising causes of conflict comes from the way different people perceive the same event. Policemen and insurance companies know that witnesses can give varying accounts of the same accident. Their perceptions can vary dramatically. In fact, perception differences are so common that we live with them every day.

A father of a six-month-old baby is met at home by a smiling wife. He perceives, "She's not done much today, except take care of the baby. I'll relax, too, and watch some TV." Behind her smile she perceives, "I've killed myself today with this child, and I'm absolutely exhausted. I'm so glad you're home because it's your turn to take care of your baby." No two people see everything alike, and it is naïve to assume that others perceive things like we do. Our human brains have different processing systems. We were not educated the same way. We have not had the same experiences. We are not processing the same data, and even if we did, we would not interpret it the same way. And no two people hold exactly the same beliefs and values.

Two women—one Anglo-American and the other African-American—attended a large Christian conference. During the conference, riots broke out in Los Angeles. The leaders of the conference, mostly white women, prayed earnestly for peace in Los Angeles. As the two women were leaving the conference, the African-American woman was so upset that she was shaking. "Why didn't they pray for justice?" she asked. "They only prayed for peace and restoring order. Doesn't anyone care about justice?" Her white friend was shocked and shaken to the core. For the first time she understood a little bit of the pain of injustice against a whole race of people.

Two friends can perceive the same conversation in totally opposite ways. With a straight face and no hint of a smile, Walter commented, "The entire world revolves around you, Dean, doesn't it? It's all about you." The comment bothered Dean because he thought that Walter really meant it as a putdown or a rebuke. So he brought it up when they got together again. Walter's perception was nowhere close to Dean's. Walter simply reminded him that Dean himself liked to joke with a straight face and no smile, and so Walter felt that gave him permission to do the same.

One fine Christian counselor reported to me that 80 to 90 percent of the marriage conflicts among his clients are perception problems. Much of what we rack up to personality conflicts may in fact come from how people perceive their differences with others. Little wonder that those who specialize in mediation spend so much time on accurate communication between the adversaries. How can we resolve our problems if we do not understand each other? How can we understand if we perceive things in such dissimilar ways? How can we find a common solution if we do not even grasp what is really tearing up the emotions of the other person? Two people can work together quite well even if they disagree, but they cannot if they misunderstand each other.

Identity Differences

We would add a fourth category—the differences in identity. Some find their identity in ability, wealth, appearance or intelligence. Others find it in their job or family relationships. Around the world some find it in their nation, race, tribe or language. For all who belong to our Lord Jesus, their deepest identity is in Christ. We are children of God, new creations in Christ, members of His Body. This deepest identity transcends all others. It is the defining relationship of time and eternity. It is our highest love, greatest good and fiercest loyalty. It surpasses our identity as citizens of our country, as men and women, as parents and children. It is far greater than beauty, brains or talent.

From our identity in Christ emerges our deepest convictions, beliefs that cannot be compromised. For centuries Christians have chosen death over denying Jesus as Lord. In the Old Testament, God's people found their deepest identity in the Sovereign Lord God. For them, as for us, this identity is so crucial because we will become like the God we worship and serve. In fact, much of God's conflict with His people in Old Testament times came from their identifying with idols. Worshiping and serving these false gods led them into immoral lifestyles, social injustice and inhumane practices (even offering their children in the fire to false gods).

Conflicts based on our identity as a child of God are the most costly of all. Think of a few examples from the Bible:

- Elijah challenged the prophets of Baal to a power encounter, and God answered with fire from heaven. His opponent, Queen Jezebel, hunted him as a criminal.
- Paul refused to make physical circumcision and Jewish law-keeping a requirement for Gentiles to become Christians. His opponents hounded him for the rest of his ministry.
- Jesus refused to give way to the pressure of the Pharisees, who wanted him to uphold the "traditions of the elders" and stop claiming that He was the Messiah. His opponents crucified Him.

Our Lord Jesus not only faced conflict about who He was, His deepest identity as the Son of God, but He also predicted that His followers would receive the same brutal treatment. Some conflicts are not only unavoidable, they are inevitable. This was what Jesus was talking about when He said,

Do not suppose that I have come to bring peace to the earth. I did not come to bring peace, but a sword. For I have come to turn "a man against his father, a daughter against her mother, a daughter-in-law against her mother-in-law—a man's enemies will be the members of his own household" (Matt. 10:34).

Identity in Christ goes deeper than the closest family relationships!

"In fact, everyone who wants to live a godly life in Christ Jesus will be persecuted" (2 Tim. 3:12). It will come true for you, if you dare pay the price. This is not for wimps, whiners or crybabies. Why don't we have our Sunday School children memorize this verse? It would put steel in their souls for the trouble they will face for standing up for Jesus and His truth.

If we want to live trouble-free lives while serving Christ, we can expect defeat. If we avoid the agony, we will miss the glory.

> **IF WE AVOID THE AGONY, WE WILL MISS THE GLORY.**

We can save our lives, but only to lose them. Jesus said, "If anyone would come after me, he must deny himself and take up his cross daily and follow me. For whoever wants to save his life will lose it, but whoever loses his life for me will save it" (Luke 9:23-24). If we choose to follow Jesus, we should not be shocked when it leads to conflict and persecution.

Do not be surprised about the loss of prestige, a desired promotion or much-wanted popularity. Do not be surprised by the cutting remarks, little put-downs and loss of certain friends. Do not be surprised by the pressure from family members to conform to the ways of this world. And do not be overwhelmed by the toll in time, money and energy that Christian service takes.

It is so easy to offer excuses: I'm burned out. This is more than I bargained for. Nobody told me it would be this rough. I think I'll hang it up and do something else for a while. What's the use? It's hopeless.

If persecution, the inevitable conflict created by following Jesus, really hurts—and it will—ask some tough questions: Am I better than Jesus? Do I deserve better treatment than He received? If they crucified Him, won't they persecute me?

In some countries today, such as North Korea, Sudan and Bhutan, persecution of Christians is physical and brutal. To openly convert to Christianity is to court disaster, deprivation or even death. Statisticians such as David Barrett tell us that the twentieth century had more martyrs than the first 19 combined. The twenty-first century could well be the bloodiest yet for followers of Christ.

The good news is that after the pain and pressure our heavenly Father always brings a rescue to the faithful followers of His Son. After lethal Friday comes Easter Sunday. After crucifixion comes resurrection. After death comes life. Sometimes rescue or relief comes in this life, sometimes not until the next. Sometimes conflicts find resolution, relationships improve, reconciliation occurs. But not always. Sometimes the struggles just go on and on and on. Whatever the outcome, God is always just. He will reward the faithful who live godly lives in Christ Jesus. And His rewards of grace far outweigh the pain of persecution. He gives life, love, joy, peace, patience and contentment (see John 10:10; Gal. 5:22-23; 1 Tim. 6:6). He recognizes us, rewards us for faithful service, honors us as fellow heirs of the grace of life and glorifies us in eternity.

It is worth the loss of prestige, promotion or popularity in order to hear those priceless words on that final judgment day: "Well done, good and faithful servant! You have been faithful with a few things; I will put you in charge of many things. Come and share your master's happiness!" (Matt. 25:23). The eternal gain is worth more than the temporal pain. "For our light and momentary troubles are achieving for us an eternal glory that far outweighs them all" (2 Cor. 4:17).

CONFLICT-PRONE PEOPLE

It is impossible to understand conflict without realizing that people are often the problem! Some people are conflict prone while others are reconciliation prone. Some are problem producers while others are problem solvers. Almost every extended family, church or company has one or more conflict-prone people. Trouble follows them wherever they go. They constantly antagonize those around them, resulting in bitter squabbles. The book of Proverbs says, "A hot-tempered man stirs up dissension, but a patient man calms a quarrel" (15:18), and "Reckless words pierce like a sword, but the tongue of the wise brings healing" (12:18).

Personality factors, genetics and family-of-origin environment all play a part in discovering differences between conflict-prone and reconciliation-prone people. Before we jump to judgment about them, we do well to reflect on their painful pasts. Henry Wadsworth Longfellow once wrote, "If we could read the secret history of our enemies, we should find in each person's life sorrow and suffering enough to disarm all hostility."[5] Whatever the causes, most extended families and all kinds of groups have both conflict-prone and reconciliation-prone people. Notice how each kind of person treats you.

Reconciliation-Prone	Conflict-Prone
Notices you	Ignores you
Affirms you	Criticizes you
Wants the best for you	Wants what you have
Gives to you	Takes from you
Serves you	Expects more from you
Honors you	Uses you
Forgives you	Resents you
Loves you	Abuses you
Stands up for you	Deserts you
Sacrifices for you	Abandons you

Note: Observe conduct during and after a conflict, not when everything is going well.

The good news of the gospel is that conflict-prone people are not hopeless. Some do turn around and become peacemakers and reconcilers. Some simply grow up. Some go through the Steps to Freedom or encounter Christ in some fresh way that includes repentance and faith. Some gain new insights into themselves through counseling or a high-accountability group. Some experience a life-threatening situation or near-death experience that forever changes their outlook. Some face the possibility of an overwhelming loss if they do not turn around their behavior and start treating others better. God's grace extends to everyone.

Even though people sometimes do change their destructive behaviors, it does not always negate the sad consequences of self-centered living. Sinful arrogance and selfishness cause conflict, but we can find a better way to live. Think of some examples from the Bible:

- King David committed adultery with Uriah's wife. Conflict never left his family after that day. But revolutionary repentance removed the consequence of his own death penalty—the punishment from God that David deserved for his deliberate adultery and conspiracy to murder (2 Sam. 12:13-14).
- James and John wanted to call down fire from heaven when their enemies snubbed them. Jesus rebuked them and avoided the conflict (see Luke 9:51-56).
- Paul and Barnabas disagreed sharply about whether to add Mark to the team for their next missions trip. They split up and formed two missions teams, one with Mark and one without him (see Acts 15:36-41).

In each of these cases, those who dealt best with the conflict used spiritual weapons. Later chapters deal with problems and processes, but we need to consider first the personal problems of sin and deception and the role the struggle in the heavenly realms might play (see Eph. 6:12). When we deal with conflict-prone people in godly ways, we disarm the unseen forces of evil all over again, or, more accurately, we expose them as already stripped of their weapons (see Col. 2:15).

We need to seek a biblical balance concerning spiritual warfare. Some see swarms of demons attacking people from the outside, like invisible aliens from a distant planet. Others see nothing at all and buy into this world's view that our conflicts are all physical and/or psychological. Both views are inadequate and incomplete. The biblical pattern is that the roots of conflict lie within us, within our flesh, springing from our evil desires. But the evil one quickly takes advantage of any foothold of sin or rotten attitude in our lives.

The battle for the mind is Satan's primary weapon, both in conflict-prone people and in those who suffer from their selfish tactics. The evil one uses tempting thoughts, accusing thoughts, deceiving thoughts. Sometimes he utilizes discouraging, doubting or disillusioning thoughts. Paul warned: "The Spirit clearly says that in later times some will abandon the faith and follow deceiving spirits and things taught by demons" (1 Tim. 4:1). Often these deceiving thoughts are perceived to be harmless self-talk, so we falsely believe they are accurate and just.

A sure way to lose in any conflict is to fight with the world's weapons (see 2 Cor. 10:3-5). Defensiveness. Blaming. Finger-pointing. Withdrawal. Abandonment. Anger. Rage. Violence. Fear. Self-indulgence. Conflict-prone personalities use these tactics. But a sure way to win the spiritual battle behind any human conflict is to fight with spiritual weapons. The Bible speaks of "weapons of righteousness in the right hand and in the left" (2 Cor. 6:7). The right hand was for an offensive weapon, such as a sword; the left hand was for a defensive weapon, such as a shield (or vice versa if you were left-handed).

Defensive weapons include right thoughts, true thoughts, to counter evil ones. Our offensive weapon is God's Word, in the wisdom and power of God's Spirit, to answer false reasoning. Meditate long and hard on 2 Timothy 2:24-26 and its relationship to spiritual warfare, as emphasized below:

> The Lord's servant must not quarrel; instead, he must be *kind to everyone, able to teach,* not resentful. Those who oppose him he must *gently instruct,* in the *hope* that God will grant them *repentance* leading them to *a knowledge of the truth,* and that they will come to their senses and escape from the trap of the devil, who has taken them captive to do his will (emphasis added).

Spiritual weapons include "purity, understanding, patience and kindness" (2 Cor. 6:6). We use them "in the Holy Spirit and in sincere love; in truthful speech and in the power of God" (vv. 6-7). The full armor of God includes truth, righteousness, readiness of the gospel of peace, faith, salvation, the Word of God (see Eph. 6:14-18).

Winning the battle for the mind is not only the best defense against the evil one, but also the best way to avoid being used or abused by conflict-prone people. Speaking the truth in love is the best offense. Only in Christ and by the power of the Holy Spirit can we fight with these powerful spiritual weapons that tear down strongholds of conflict and disrupt the schemes of the devil behind them.

CHAPTER 8

PATTERNS OF CONFLICT

*We all need to get on the same end of this rope and
pull in the same direction. If we do, nobody can
defeat us in the long run.*

Tommy Lasorda

Some conflicts make us laugh, others make us cry. This one
came as an unsolicited e-mail. It is good for a laugh.

MEMO
FROM: Patty Lewis, Human Resources Director
TO: All Employees
RE: Christmas Party
DATE: December 5

I'm happy to inform you that the company Christmas
Party will take place on December 23, starting at noon in
the banquet room at Luigi's Open Pit Barbecue. No bar,
but plenty of eggnog! We'll have a small band playing
traditional carols—feel free to sing along. And don't be
surprised if our CEO shows up dressed as Santa Claus!
A Christmas tree will be lit at 1:00 P.M. Exchange of gifts
among employees can be done then; however, no gift
should be over $10.00 to make the giving of gifts easy for

everyone. This gathering is only for employees! A special announcement will be made by our CEO at that time!

Merry Christmas to you and your family,

Patty

MEMO
FROM: Patty Lewis, Human Resources Director
TO: All Employees
RE: Holiday Party
DATE: December 6

In no way was yesterday's memo intended to exclude our Jewish employees. We recognize that Chanukah is an important holiday which often coincides with Christmas, although unfortunately not this year. However, from now on we're calling it our "Holiday Party." The same policy applies to employees who are celebrating Kwanzaa at this time. There will be no Christmas tree present. No Christmas carols sung. We will have other types of music for your enjoyment. Happy now?

Happy Holidays to you and your family,

Patty

MEMO
FROM: Patty Lewis, Human Resources Director
TO: All Employees
RE: Holiday Party
DATE: December 7

What a diverse group we are! I had no idea that December 20 begins the Muslim holy month of

Ramadan, which forbids eating and drinking during daylight hours. There goes the party! Seriously, we can appreciate how a luncheon this time of year does not accommodate our Muslim employees' beliefs. Perhaps Luigi's can hold off on serving your meal until the end of the party—the days are so short this time of year--or else package everything for take-home in little foil swans. Will that work? Meanwhile I've arranged for members of Overeaters Anonymous to sit farthest from the dessert buffet and pregnant women will get the table closest to the restrooms. We will have booster seats for short people.

Sorry! Did I miss anything?

Patty

MEMO
FROM: Patty Lewis, Human Resources Director
TO: All Employees
DATE: December 8
RE: Holiday Party

So December 22 marks the Winter Solstice . . . what do you expect me to do, a tap-dance on your heads? Fire regulations at Luigi's prohibit the burning of sage by our "earth-based, goddess-worshiping" employees, but we'll try to accommodate your drumming circle during the band's breaks.

Could we lighten up? Please?????????? The company has also changed its mind in announcing the special announcement at the gathering. You will get a notification in the mail sent to your home.

Patty

MEMO
FROM: Patty Lewis, Human Resources Director
TO: All Idiotic Employees
DATE: December 9
RE: The Stupid Holiday Party

I haven't the slightest idea what the CEO's announcement is all about. Why do I care anyway???? I KNOW
WHAT I AM GOING TO GET!!!!!!! You change your
address now and you are dead!!!!!!!!!! No more changes
of address will be allowed in my office. Try to come in
and change your address, I will have you hung from the
ceiling in the warehouse!!!!!!!!!!

Vegetarians!?!?!? I've had it with you people!!! We're
going to keep this party at Luigi's Open Pit Barbecue
whether you like it or not, so you can sit quietly at the table
furthest from the "grill of death" as you so quaintly put it,
and you'll get your salad bar, including hydroponic tomatoes. But you know, they have feelings too. Tomatoes
scream when you slice them. I've heard them scream. I'm
hearing them scream right now! HA! I hope you all have a
rotten holiday! Drive drunk and die, you hear me!!!!!!!!!!

Ms. Grinch!!!

MEMO
FROM: Terry Bishop, Acting Human Resources Director
TO: All Employees
DATE: December 14
RE: Patty Lewis and the Holiday Party

I'm sure I speak for all of us in wishing Patty Lewis a
speedy recovery from her stress-related illness, and I'll

continue to forward your cards to her at the sanitarium. In the meantime, management has decided to cancel our Holiday Party and give everyone the afternoon of the 23rd off with full pay.

Happy Holidays!

Beliefs, values and attitudes lie at the heart of conflict, and problems take on a life of their own, especially in groups. They form into patterns, almost predictable in their healthy or unhealthy development. Although they seem so different, in reality, the structures of human conflict are remarkably similar.

The dynamics of change create new needs. These in turn produce new desires. Some welcome the proposed changes, but others resist them. Not all changes are good; in fact, many are harmful, even evil. Differing desires lead to collisions, clashes and conflicts. These differences may be as mild as mere preferences or as serious as the wrath of God against His people's stubborn refusal to change their thinking and their ways.

Every miracle in the Bible began with human suffering and people in conflict. Every dramatic answer to prayer came in a time of trouble—the Exodus from Egypt, the crossing of the Red Sea, the wall of Jericho. Recall Gideon with his lamps and trumpets before the Midianites, David with his sling before Goliath, Elijah with his prayer of faith before the prophets of Baal. Consider the ministries of the prophets and apostles and Jesus Himself. The Bible is a record of human failure and God's redemption. Consider a sampling of 10 kinds of disputes:

Issue	People	Reference
Sin	Adam and Eve	Gen. 3
Property	Abram and Lot	Gen. 13
Jealousy	Joseph and brothers	Gen. 37; 42—45

Authority	Miriam and Aaron	Num. 12
Sexism	Zelophehad's daughters	Num. 27; 36
Deception	Ananias and Sapphira	Acts 5:1-10
Conscience	Weaker and stronger	Rom. 14
Racism	Jews and Gentiles	Eph. 2:11-22
Disagreement	Euodia and Syntyche	Phil. 4:2-3
Elitism	Philemon and Onesimus	Philem. 8-22

So often conflict brings suffering, and the inspired writers of the Bible with one voice affirm that we can expect suffering as part of God's plan. "Many are the afflictions of the righteous," observed David (Ps. 34:19, *NASB*). "In this world you will have trouble," Jesus predicted (John 16:33). James assumes his readers will "face trials of many kinds" (Jas. 1:2). A heart set free from inner turmoil never depends on serene circumstances—never, never, never. Every problem and conflict leads to a decision. The tough times force a choice—to become a better person or a worse one. Character either matures or crumbles depending on the response to God while the pressure is on. Conflicts reveal our character.

A bedrock principle in the Bible is that God uses evil, actual evil, to produce something good (see Gen. 50:20). The informed Christian knows God's promise that in everything, no matter how tragic it appears, God is working for our good. "And we know that in all things God works for the good of those who love him, who have been called according to his purpose" (Rom. 8:28). A group of pastors and leaders developed time lines of their lives as part of a Refocusing Leaders seminar. In reflecting on the charts, they noticed an intriguing truth. The greatest lessons came from the hardest times. What God taught them after painful conflict molded their ministries more than what they learned in the more comfortable periods. Even undeserved criticism and bitter injustices led to new insights into people and ministry.

CYCLES OF CONFLICT

Conflicts vary widely as to how severe they are. It makes a huge difference whether the conflict stems from mere preferences, varied roles, imperfect perception, cherished values, biblical truth or our deepest identity in Christ. Some conflicts include material issues, such as money, property, child custody, border disputes or water rights. Nearly all conflicts include personality factors, such as attitudes and people skills—or lack of them! Destructive conflicts occur among people crippled by selfishness, sin and satanic influence. Constructive conflicts build people who rely on God's wisdom and creativity along with healthy processes. The goal is to turn potential disaster into a greater good.

Conflict is as devious as sin itself. It can take a hundred faces and a thousand forms. But a typical cycle in families, churches, communities and nations might look something like the pattern below. Destructive and constructive conflicts follow similar cycles but take different directions as they develop.

Constructive Conflicts	**Destructive Conflicts**
Open tensions	Hidden tensions
Discussion about conflict	Gossip about conflict
Huddle for "win-win"	Choose up sides for "win-lose"
Honor persons and processes	Go to war
Come to unity	Cause division
Move forward together	Conform or get out
New tensions emerge	New tensions emerge

The typical cycle will repeat itself as long as we work with people.[1] In fact, conflict is so common that it may help us to think of ourselves in fresh ways—as Christ's ambassadors in conflict, peacemakers, ministers of reconciliation (see Matt. 5:9; 2 Cor. 5:14-21). Conflict brings opportunity, stimulates creativity, and often brings out the best or worst in people. It is worth examining the two cycles step by step.

Open Tensions Versus Hidden Tensions

Constructive and destructive conflicts both begin with differences and tensions. What makes a difference is how people handle them. Constructive conflicts no longer lurk in the shadows but move into the light. Open tensions move toward resolution while hidden ones fester and spread bitterness. So why do people keep them hidden? Some do not want to be known as whiners and crybabies. Some prefer the art of manipulation. Some love juicy gossip. Some know what they are doing is wrong, and they prefer to stay out of sight.

When the causes of tension are grievous enough, intervention becomes necessary. Especially when the pain spreads to people around us, we dare not remain silent. Sometimes it is wiser to precipitate a small crisis than to wait for a big explosion. At other times it pays to appeal to those in authority about something that needs to be addressed. On many occasions a quiet, loving confrontation does more good than walking away in frustration and anger.

But sometimes not! Every rule has an exception. Many tensions need to be released in private. Alone before God, the hurt person forgives the offender from the heart—and never brings the subject up again. In good marriages, good companies and good churches, people constantly put up with each other's weaknesses and faults. In fact, they cover for each other, pick up the fumbled football and run interference. The Bible clearly teaches this principle of overlooking offenses:

- Bear with each other and forgive whatever grievances you may have against one another. Forgive as the Lord forgave you (Col. 3:13).

- Above all, love each other deeply, because love covers over a multitude of sins (1 Pet. 4:8).
- He who covers over an offense promotes love, but whoever repeats the matter separates close friends (Prov. 17:9).

The Bible constantly points to love as the crown jewel of the virtues. Love keeps us out of many conflicts, teaches us how to handle the others. Love knows when to look the other way, and when to confront. Love sees the underlying cause of tension and addresses it tenderly. Love searches for wholesome healing words and avoids demeaning critical ones. The love chapter in the Bible says love "keeps no record of wrongs" (1 Cor. 13:5). Instead of demonizing those who cause the tensions, love reflects God's own compassionate heart toward sinners. "It always protects, always trusts, always hopes, always perseveres" (v. 7).

> **THE BIBLE CONSTANTLY POINTS TO LOVE AS THE CROWN JEWEL OF THE VIRTUES.**

Discussion About Conflict Versus Gossip About Conflict

In healthy conflict, those in leadership listen to complaints, and those who are unhappy talk to the right people. A simple rule for constructive conflicts is: Talk to the right person in the right spirit. The right person is the one involved in the problem, and the right spirit is a learner's attitude. Tons of trouble and many lawsuits will be avoided when the grieved person talks candidly with the perceived offender. One attorney for plaintiffs in employment disputes said he likes to phone the company attorney right from the beginning. "We have a problem here. Would you like to meet and talk it over before this situation moves into legal action?" Usually they do meet and often a good solution is worked out without a court battle.

We (Chuck and Neil) have both served as senior pastors and as associate pastors. In the role of associate pastors, over and over again some people would make complaints to us about the senior pastor or other staff, hoping that we would lobby for their cause. At times it felt like manipulation. A good question was "Have you talked with the senior pastor about it?" The answer usually was "No, I can't talk to him, but he'll listen to you."

"I really think you should talk to him." And if we wanted to add a little weight to our request, we added, "I'll be seeing him before long, and I'll tell him that you would like to talk with him."

"Oh, no, no! Don't do that." Some would then back off and drop the issue. A few others responded to the biblical challenge. They were more than gripers and grumblers. What bothered them was serious enough to talk with the right person, in this case the senior pastor. The result most often was that they came away relieved and satisfied. While sometimes the issue was not fully resolved, it remained on the table for further discussion.

Missionaries and students of cross-cultural conflict point out that major differences exist in how various people groups handle tense disagreements. Some focus more on the individual and others more on the group—me-cultures and we-cultures. In me-cultures, such as in the United States and Europe, people need to move from denial or avoidance to loving confrontation. Me-cultures are more individualized and focus on personal rights, desires and needs. So conflicts often are worked out face-to-face. (Please do not misunderstand. Neither kind of culture is necessarily better than the other.)

In the teaching of Jesus, the classic passage for resolving conflict is Matthew 18:15-17:

> If your brother sins against you, go and show him his
> fault, just between the two of you. If he listens to you,
> you have won your brother over. But if he will not listen,
> take one or two others along, so that "every matter may
> be established by the testimony of two or three witness-
> es." If he refuses to listen to them, tell it to the church;
> and if he refuses to listen even to the church, treat him
> as you would a pagan or a tax collector.

The first step of Jesus' teaching in Matthew 18:15-17 takes on special importance in me-cultures, "just between the two of you" (v. 15).

In a we-culture, such as most traditional cultures in the non-Western world, people need to save face and restore group harmony. We-cultures are more others oriented and focus on common interests and protection. So conflict often works out indirectly through intermediaries, trusted friends and respected elders. The first step of Matthew 18 is important but may seem extremely indirect to an outside observer. The second step is the crucial one in we-cultures: "But if he will not listen, take one or two others along" (v. 16). In fact, in many we-cultures the normal pattern is to send the two or three as negotiators, message-carriers, peacemakers, while the antagonists stay apart.

In both me-cultures and we-cultures, when the discussion of conflict is opened in appropriate ways, everything tends to move in a better direction. But if the discussion goes on mainly through gossip channels, watch out for trouble ahead. In all cultures gossip is deadly. False assumptions, innuendo and half-truths can decimate friendships and undermine leadership. Proverbs warns about gossip again and again: "Without wood a fire goes out; without gossip a quarrel dies down" (26:20), and "A perverse man stirs up dissension, and a gossip separates close friends" (16:28; see also 11:13; 18:8; 20:19; 26:22).

Most often gossips are looking for support or for allies. What is frustrating is that gossips seldom want to resolve conflict in a healthy way. They prefer the attention that comes from hints of slander, choice tidbits of inside information, humor at someone else's expense. Many church leaders in the past few years have worked through the *Setting Your Church Free* process.[2] One of the most common corporate sins many leaders have identified and renounced in their own churches is gossip!

Huddle for Win-Win Versus Choose Sides for Win-Lose

Conflicts have three possible outcomes: win-win, win-lose or lose-lose. Even children understand the difference between a win-win conflict and a win-lose fight. A win-win situation allows both parties in the conflict to leave feeling good. They won something, even if it was only the opportunity to get a point across. Often the disputants reach a mutually satisfactory agreement and begin working together. It is worth all the effort to pursue a win-win solution.

A flashing red light, warning that conflict is about to explode, comes when people in a group begin choosing sides for a win-lose scenario. This is the time, not later, for the leaders and peacemakers in the group to start looking for outside help. Choosing sides is unclean, a monster in the making, a battle looming. What lies ahead is disaster, although many will not yet know it. When people start choosing sides it is time for some wise insights, gentle persuasion, even intervention. An outside mediator or a leader in a position of authority can often make a big difference at this stage. Unfortunately, if no explosion has taken place, many in the group think they can handle it on their own. The biggest complaint by church superintendents and interventionists is that the disputants wait too long before calling for help.

Ask the wisest people you know how to proceed, what to avoid, when to speak. Someone experienced in conflict resolution can bring the core issues to the surface at this stage, and sometimes guide toward full reconciliation.

A few blustery types will argue that they do not want to pussyfoot around. They wave the flag for battle and rally the troops for war. A strange earthquake fault line in our depraved thinking is that the strongest people lead into battle and the milquetoasts work for peace. Actually it is just the opposite. Reconciliation comes when the wisest, most persuasive, most forceful personalities put their energies into making peace. Remember Jesus' beatitude: "Blessed are the peacemakers, for they will be called sons of God" (Matt. 5:9).

> RECONCILIATION COMES WHEN THE WISEST, MOST PERSUASIVE, MOST FORCEFUL PERSONALITIES PUT THEIR ENERGIES INTO MAKING PEACE. REMEMBER JESUS' BEATITUDE: "BLESSED ARE THE PEACEMAKERS, FOR THEY WILL BE CALLED SONS OF GOD."

People who rush into conflict do great damage—to themselves and to the whole group. They forget the vital first step of talking with the right person in the right spirit. Or they talk but do not fully perceive the other's point of view. Or they answer before they listen, unwilling to find reasonable alternatives. "He who answers before listening—that is his folly and his shame" (Prov. 18:13). "Reckless words pierce like a sword, but the tongue of the wise brings healing" (Prov. 12:18).

In healthy conflict, however, people on both sides of the table are exploring options, praying for guidance, suggesting possible solutions. Well-run businesses or churches have a track record of resolving previous conflicts. Their attitude is that we have resolved, or at least gotten past, conflicts before—and we will work our way through this one. Their trust is in the Lord, not in their own ability. They live for His glory and do not want to disgrace His name. They want the best for their company, community or church, as well as for the people involved in the dispute. Be warned: People with good intentions can fall into poor patterns. Good intentions alone will not keep individuals or groups out of destructive conflict.

Honor People and Processes Versus Go to War

In a constructive conflict, healthy discussion is going on, both among those who agree and those who disagree. All are exploring options and possible solutions. They are trying to avoid a severe collision or to disarm the antagonists so that they will inflict only minor damage on each other. In *A Shepherd Looks at Psalm 23,*[3] Philip Keller tells the humorous reality of rams entering furious battles for the favors of the ewes during the season of the rut, mating time. They can actually damage or even kill one another as they butt heads! So as a smart shepherd, he put generous amounts of axle grease on the horns and noses of the rams. Then when they collided they slipped off each other and stood there looking silly, not knowing quite what to do next!

Keller makes his application to the presence and ministry of the Holy Spirit among believers. Right on. We would add that the Lord's undershepherds can also add grease by honoring the people involved and by being very careful to follow agreed-upon processes. Prayer, personal counsel and a lot of love cause antagonists to look silly instead of tough!

In terms of honoring people, it helps to assign the best motives to our critics, not the worst ones. The evil one, and our own fleshly desires, conspire to tempt us to define the identity of those who oppose us by this dispute alone. In reality, the others are complex people with joys and heartaches of their own. This conflict may be killing them, too.

In terms of process, church polity, the company's personnel handbook, the mediator's rules—or whatever process rightly fits the situation—simply must be honored. People who cannot get their way legitimately will often attack their opponents for violating the process. So walking carefully here prevents stumbling later on.

In a destructive conflict the two sides go to war. Some fight fair, others fight dirty. It is amazing how devoted Christians will lose sight of their true identity when a conflict erupts into an explosion. Some later feel ashamed of their conduct and regret that it was nothing that brought glory or honor to their Lord Jesus. Some repent deeply and go to their brothers and sisters to be reconciled. Others simply feel that the ends justified the means, that nasty business is sometimes necessary and that on some occasions Christ's teachings are not very practical. May the Lord have mercy upon them when they stand before the judgment seat of Christ and receive what is due them, whether good or bad (see 2 Cor. 5:10).

Come to Unity Versus Cause Division
By this time, those moving along the path of healthy conflict are examining a variety of possible solutions. Or they may have settled on one that is mutually agreeable. Through prayer, discussion and seeking the mind of Christ, they reach unity and move ahead. The creativity of this process never ceases to amaze us. God's grace has an infinite variety of patterns in moving toward Christ-centered reconciliation. It is astounding how innovative people can become when they decide to cooperate.

In healthy churches and organizations, certain assumed procedures take place—both formally and informally. Some people exercise their gifts of wisdom, discernment and mercy. Others lead with authority and a servant's heart, much as our Lord did. Most follow cultural patterns learned as children, or the particular subculture of the denomination, corporation or volunteer group.

> **MOST OFTEN IT IS AFTER THE WAR HAS BROKEN OUT AND BULLETS ARE FLYING THAT THE COMBATANTS START CALLING IN REINFORCEMENTS.**

By this time those moving along the path of unhealthy conflict are in a win-lose collision. The other side is definitely filled with the bad guys and our side has the good guys. Each side has its demands, and usually the alternatives are incompatible. Stubbornness, refusal to listen, demonizing opponents, defense of our "honor," and a number of ingenious tricks sneak into play. It is a deadly game, and many will get hurt. War always causes casualties. Unfortunately, some of those who suffer the most are the innocent ones in the middle, who never wanted the conflict in the first place.

Most often it is after the war has broken out and bullets are flying that the combatants start calling in reinforcements. Sometimes both sides will want outside help from those in authority, but both expect that authority to support their cause and crush the other. It takes remarkable skill for interventionists or outside consultants to make any significant difference at this stage. However, skilled mediators can sometimes make a big difference. Look for people of peace to calm the quarrel!

Move Forward Together Versus Conform or Get Out

At the end of the process, constructive conflict produces reconciliation between people and often a mutually satisfactory solution to the problem. All three elements of the conflict—people,
problems and process—have worked their way through to an
acceptable conclusion. Life is never perfect, and so some people
may in fact leave the group, church or business. Given a little
time, others get over their hurts and bruises and return to life as
it was before the conflict. However, it will never be the same,
because most often it will be better. The creativity and effort put
into reconciliation met real needs, rose to fresh challenges, created new solutions and built up the participants in Christ. In
healthy groups with good leadership and the presence of the
Holy Spirit, it happens all the time.

Destructive conflict most often finishes the fight with a
win-lose scenario. One side crushes the opposition and demands submission and conformity. The only alternative is to
get out of the group or church or voluntary organization. In
companies and corporations, heads have rolled by this point—
some fired, others reassigned or transferred to another part of
the country. The task now is to get over it and get on with life.
Some find this relatively easy, especially the bullies and bruisers.
They are ready for the next battle. Others find it nearly impossible to recover. They internalize the pain and carry the scars
with them for a lifetime.

New Tensions Emerge Versus New Tensions Emerge

The surprise to both sides is that harmony does not last. As situations and people change, differing desires emerge again.
Often these create pressures for change that some want and others do not. So conflict will come back again, either in constructive or destructive patterns.

- The myth is that harmony is permanent. The truth is that harmony is temporary.
- The myth is that conflict is deplorable. The truth is that conflict is essential.
- The myth is that someone is to blame for causing conflict. The truth is that all need to lay down their lives in love to resolve differences.
- The myth is that solutions are final. The truth is that solutions last only as long as the situation, and people stay the same, often not for long.
- The myth is that conflict is always sin. The truth is that conflict is God's opportunity for reconciliation.[4]

CONFLICT AND CHARACTER

What really complicates conflict is character flaws. It is not just disagreement, even disputes on the toughest issues, that makes conflict so painful. It is when our character weaknesses come through. Those of us who are married understand this quite well. No one has a perfect husband, perfect wife or perfect marriage. The best marriages hurt some of the time, and the worst ones hurt almost all of the time.

When serious conflict emerges, the kind that is difficult to resolve, it is no fun. It brings out the worst in people, and yet sometimes it can bring out the best. What builds a great life is character, and character does not come easily (see Rom. 5:3-4). It comes from tribulation and perseverance—having a Christlike attitude as you put up with troubles for a long time. It comes from forbearance, living with another's weaknesses even though they grate on our nerves. It comes from forgiveness—releasing the offense, letting it go and starting over. It comes from responding to unfairness with kindness. It comes from trying to make the best of a difficult situation. It comes from enduring suffering and trouble that we did not ask for and cannot prevent.

Character also comes from humbling ourselves, taking a painful look at our own faults and sins, admitting we were wrong, asking forgiveness, making things right, working out the difficulty, communicating with the intent of solving it. Character compels us to do something about the problem. It calls for wisdom: Should I speak up or shut up? Act now or act later? Go to work or sit back? Give in or hang tough? Change attitude or change course?

Nothing builds character like living in Christ. Nothing tests character like conflict. Nothing shows whether or not we are really living in Christ like how we work out the conflicts and resolve the troubles in marriage and family, at work and play, in the community and the church. My mom used to say that the hardest place to live the Christian life was at home. She insisted that if we could live it at home, we could live it anywhere. She was so right.

When you ask Christ to make you a problem solver, you are really asking Him to remodel your character. That is tough. It requires suffering, patience, perseverance, forgiveness, wisdom, love and self-control. In the end, however, character produces confidence. It produces confidence in Christ and confidence in His character within us. That confidence gives us hope for the future and hope for our conflicts. No wonder we want the Lord to build His character in us.

WHEN CONFLICT FIRST STRIKES

We can't always choose the conflicts that come into our lives,
but we can choose our responses to those conflicts.

Carolyn Schrock-Shenk, *Making Peace with Conflict*

It seems to come out of nowhere—the verbal bombshell that causes such emotional turmoil.

At home: "I've decided I don't want to be married anymore. I'm filing for divorce."

On a voice message: "I know you're out of town and this is not a good time, but Melissa didn't come home last night. I tried to phone you, but your cell phone must be turned off. I called the police about 2:00 A.M., but they won't do anything for 24 hours. She finally showed up this morning just before I went to work and wouldn't talk. What are we going to do? She's only 16! You need to come home right away."

At work: "I'm sorry, but we are terminating you. The problems we discussed in your last few performance reviews haven't been resolved. You have 15 minutes to clean out your desk and turn in your keys."

At church: "I don't care if the pastor's kids are in the group— I can't stand drums and guitars in Sunday morning worship! We're bringing the world into the church! Maybe it's time for a new pastor."

From school: "This is the vice principal calling. We're suspending Mike for three days. Our zero-tolerance policy on illegal drugs has no exceptions. We are obligated by law to report his possession of narcotics to the police."

Behind each of these conversations, dissatisfaction was already brewing, but we did not know it was that bad! The friction, the disrespect, the coolness, the anger—all the telltale signs were present. We should have seen it coming! Is it too late? Can we restore this relationship, save this marriage, find a better job, win back the adolescent? What do we do now?

FIRST BLOWS

Our first reaction under sudden and shocking stress is emotional: Freeze from shock. Cry. Withdraw. Run. Get mad. Fight. Quit. Give up. Give in. Hit back. Blame. Accuse. Get even. Get defensive. Blow up. Scream. Go silent. Those who know us well can predict our response, and try to steer clear of us. Others will try to bring comfort or relief:

"I'm so sorry."

"You didn't deserve this."

"It's not your fault."

"I would feel exactly the same way."

"Would it be alright if I prayed for you?"

But the conflict does not go away; in fact, sometimes it gets worse—a lot worse—and our comforters back off. Some blame us and make life more miserable by becoming our critics. They see our worst side and point it out to others instead of talking with us. Or they let us know in no uncertain terms how we fouled up their lives, disappointed them, let them down. They are the peace-breakers.

Some grow cool, give us too much space, distance themselves from us. They do not want to get involved. They are peace-fakers.

But a few hang in there, stand by us, give us good counsel, refuse to fight or run, keep praying earnestly for us and for the other one in the conflict. They are the peacemakers.

It is what comes next that counts—what we do after the first blows. Churning thoughts, fitful sleep, headaches, backaches, colitis, upset stomachs. Our minds spin, our emotions burn, our defense mechanisms kick in full force. We try to cope, but the blows keep coming. The other person in the conflict fills our thoughts. We cannot believe the unfair criticism, the self-justification, the twisting of facts. We thought they were Christians!

IS SATAN INVOLVED?

Christians often suspect spiritual warfare when the battle gets brutal. It is obvious that the other people are not walking with the Lord. How can they act like the devil and still claim to be Christians? At the very least, carnality reigns supreme. Our spirits are grieved over what is going on. Or in some cases, the rebellion is so blatant that we question whether they know Christ at all! Did the devil have a hand in it?

Satan loves to curse, defame, demean. He loves to disrupt, disturb, perturb. In fact, the adversary is an expert at stirring up turbulence. He orchestrates conflict, makes it worse, fights dirty, hits us at our weakest moments. His job is to wreak havoc, cause misery, rob God of His glory. What better way to make a mockery of Christian values than a nasty fight! It is at this point that the battle for the mind kicks in.

The evil one loves to put accusing thoughts into our opponents' minds during this turmoil—suspicions, doubts, assigning bad motives. Not to mention the lure of these big-time temptations behind many a contentious issue—lust and greed! It should be no surprise that Satan and his evil henchmen are stirring up lies among those on the other side of this controversy.

The surprise is that the evil one works on us and on our allies as well. He stirs up antagonism on both sides—our minds and our opponents' minds.

Stop and think. In the middle of a conflict, who has not had un-Christlike thoughts pop into his or her mind? In the heat of controversy or the pain of protracted conflict it is predictable that some kind of evil devilish thoughts and desires will come into our minds—distracting, lonely, accusing, envying, irritable, cunning, defensive, blaming, angry, resentful, bitter, unforgiving, hating, revengeful, violent, discouraging, disillusioning, overwhelming, fearful, withdrawing, criticizing, scheming, controlling, backbiting, undermining, deceiving, binding, blinding self-absorbing, tired, apathetic, drifting, disappointing, depressive, complaining, anxious, worrying, comparing, grumbling, self-pitying, condemning, gossiping, scoffing, contemptuous thoughts.

> STOP AND THINK. IN THE MIDDLE OF A CONFLICT, WHO HAS NOT HAD UN-CHRISTLIKE THOUGHTS POP INTO HIS OR HER MIND?

We are responsible for our thoughts, no matter what their initial source. Both Neil and Chuck reject a "devil made me do it" theology. If we harbor any of these thoughts and believe these lies, we are deceived. The adversary tempts us to believe we are totally right and our adversaries are totally wrong. He paints a distorted picture in our minds. We see them as all bad and ourselves as all good. The apostle of love, John, in his old age wrote in his beautiful first epistle: "If we say that we have no sin, we are deceiving ourselves, and the truth is not in us" (1 John 1:8, *NASB*). Yet the devil is not the only problem.

Self-deception enters into our thinking. Our theology tells us no one is without sin. Our common sense tells us no one is perfect. Our psychology tells us that we all have defense mechanisms. And in spite of our accurate knowledge, we still deceive ourselves with the thought, *It's all their fault!* With cunning, Satan may suggest these self-justifying thoughts come from ourselves, harmless self-talk. By the way, if they are your thoughts alone, then simply stop thinking them. But if you find that you cannot stop, suspect that the subtle schemes of the devil are also at work. The evil one loves to hide, to work in the dark. Watch out for his traps.

Our own flesh finds these thoughts comforting. We have fantasies of getting even or running away. What is more, the world system will send us "friends" who add fuel to the fire, agree with us, stir up our anger and self-justification. One of the favorite tricks of the enemy is to lead us to people who will tell us what we want to hear instead of what we need to hear. As a general guideline, look for counselors who obviously live in Christ. Look for people whom others respect and trust because of their wisdom. Seek out men and women of character, those who are kind, honest, tender, strong and pure. Avoid wimps, crybabies, whiners and moaners. Stay away from grumblers, gripers and busybodies. Read Proverbs, and look for someone who matches the Bible's description of wisdom. Pray for God to lead you to a man or woman "known to be full of the Spirit and wisdom" (Acts 6:3).

Do not forget the peacekeepers. They are the people with influence, and often authority. They set the ground rules, play referee, set the stage for reconciliation. They are men and women of peace. When they hear foolish talk they refuse to listen, change the topic of conversation or even give a mild rebuke. They often speak up with "Yes, but . . . " and offer another perspective. Because of their influence, they move people into or out of positions of honor, influence and responsibility. They motivate and inspire. Or they may organize and mobilize.

Whatever the style, these people are the leaders—and part of the job of leadership is keeping the peace. As peacekeepers walk in integrity, they become great allies in resolving conflicts and bringing about reconciliation.

When it comes to peacekeepers, do not set expectations too high. If you expect them to solve the problems for you, disillusionment is sure to set in. By necessity their primary focus is, and must be, on their area of responsibility or authority. They do not have the time to tackle everyone's conflict. After all, they have other fires burning that they must put out. But you can count on them for one visit or phone call to receive some good counsel. If your particular conflict lies within their scope of authority, their responsibility may motivate them to give much more time and attention.

WINNING THE BATTLE FOR THE MIND

When tensions build toward conflict, when you sense something is about to happen, when you get stabbed in the back, when you get clobbered without warning or when a conflict drags on and on—all of these are good times to reaffirm your identity in Christ. Claim who you are in Christ: I am a child of God. Then worship the Lord and draw near to God in prayer:

In the shock of this blow, I draw near to You, heavenly Father.
I exalt You as worthy of my praise, and determine to live for
the praise of Your glory through this crisis. Lead me today and
every day to display Your splendor, to live not for myself but for
Him who died for me and was raised again.

Open my eyes to Your majesty in creation, Your love in
redemption and Your power in the coming resurrection. Bless

*me so that I will be a blessing to my friends and foes during this
time, so that Your glory will be maximized among those who
do not know You, especially those who have never heard of
Your glorious name in a way that they could receive You.*

*I humbly welcome a living union with the presence, power, life,
work and ministry of the Lord Jesus Christ—crucified, risen,
reigning and returning. I gladly acknowledge that I am crucified, buried, made alive, raised up and seated with Christ at the
right hand of God, and I will appear with Him when He
returns to earth. I gratefully accept the reality that I'm dead to
sin, including my intense temptation to react wrongly. I affirm
that I am alive to God. I rejoice in Christ's authority to fulfill
His commands, including loving my enemies. Through faith
and obedience, overcome the evil one through me. I claim Your
promise about Satan's potential for ultimate damage—"nothing will harm you" (Luke 10:19).*

The widely used "Who I Am in Christ" applications from
God's Word are a wonderful way to reaffirm that we are accepted, secure and significant in Him (see chapter 2). Use them daily
when the pressure is on.

Affirming truths from God's written Word reminds us of our
deepest identity—we really are children of God, new creations in
Christ. They recall the promises of God. They rely on the strength
of Christ within us. They change us as we live in Christ, as we love,
trust and obey Him. What is intriguing is that these biblical
reminders give us the courage to look at ourselves from Christ's
point of view. We are loved, accepted, forgiven, affirmed, secure,
significant. We no longer see ourselves or our adversaries from a
human point of view (see 2 Cor. 5:16). We see both "them" and
"us" as in Christ, new creations, even with the old baggage of our
disillusionment with each other and divisive disagreements still

> **AFFIRMING TRUTHS FROM GOD'S WRITTEN WORD REMINDS US OF OUR DEEPEST IDENTITY— WE REALLY ARE CHILDREN OF GOD, NEW CREATIONS IN CHRIST.**

going on. We see them as brothers and sisters.

If our adversaries make no profession of Christ, even if they are openly hostile to Him, we still see them as sinners for whom Christ died. We see them as people to whom our Lord, the Suffering Servant (see Isa. 53), offers grace and forgiveness. We hold in our hands the message and ministry of reconciliation. We are Christ's ambassadors. "The one who is in you is greater than the one who is in the world" (1 John 4:4).

Through any conflict and the gracious way we handle it, we have an opportunity to share the gospel with our opponents or one of their allies who now opposes us.

STEPS TO FREEDOM

When we fully see Jesus, gazing at His holiness, and then glance at our own hearts, we are more ready to repent. This is a good time to process the Steps to Freedom. What happens is that we get very right with God. Please understand that this is not some kind of magic powder that makes everything bad go away! After going through the Steps, we will find that though the external conflict is still raging and the evil one is still attacking, we have peace with God.

When we deeply repent, search our hearts, forgive our adversaries and retake any ground given to the evil one, we are changed. When we change, the other person most often will change too—

either for the better or for the worse. It is the teeter-totter principle. If I change, the teeter-totter moves. As I lower myself in humility and heart-searching repentance before God, the other person is
lifted to new heights. It is true that some people jump off the
teeter-totter and let us go crashing to the ground again, but many
will change for the better. The closer the relationship, the more
this insight applies.

Sometimes it helps to follow scriptural practices in taking
authority over the evil one, even on a daily basis. All the versions
of the Steps to Freedom—personal, marriage, church—use biblical declarations against the evil one.[1] This is one way of using the
sword of the Spirit, the spoken Word of God, which is part of the
full armor of God mentioned in Ephesians 6:17. (The Greek
word *rhema* that is translated "word" in Ephesians 6:17 means a
spoken word. It is in contrast to the Greek word *logos*, also translated "word," which refers to the incarnate Word [see John 1:1]
or the written Word of God [see Acts 6:7]). It is important to take
our stand in Christ before engaging in any form of resisting the
enemy. For example, you might say, "In union with my Lord
Jesus Christ—crucified, risen, reigning and returning—and in His
authority, I make this declaration."

The declaration of the ancient Church is helpful: "Satan,
I renounce you in all your works and all your ways." Some like to
follow the example of Jesus during His temptation and simply
give the devil an out-loud verbal command in Christ's name,
power and authority: "Away from me, Satan!" (Matt. 4:10), or
"Begone, Satan!" (*NASB*). Still others prefer to address the evil
one indirectly by using scriptural terms: "The Lord rebuke you!"
(Jude 9); "The Lord bind you!" (see Mark 3:27). Yet others prefer
to follow Paul's teaching in Ephesians 6:10-20 and put on the
whole armor of God to wrestle "against the rulers, against the
authorities, against the powers of this dark world and against the
spiritual forces of evil in the heavenly realms" (v. 12). Whatever

the methodology, the basic promise of Scripture is still true: "Submit yourselves, then, to God. Resist the devil, and he will flee from you. Come near to God and he will come near to you" (Jas. 4:7-8).

MORE THAN "I'M SORRY"

In any conflict, a heartfelt apology goes a long way. Something about saying "I'm sorry" and meaning it does wonders in restoring a damaged relationship. Sometimes "I'm sorry" is not enough. We need a radical heart change, a deep shift in our thinking, a drastic change of our behavior. In most conflicts, this is what each wants from the other side—and each denies needing it personally!

What both Christians and non-Christians need today is *revolutionary repentance*. We know what repentance is—going one way and then turning around to go the opposite way. It is changing our thinking and our behavior. It is hating our sin the way God hates it and rejecting it with an attitude of repulsion. Most often it is accompanied by godly sorrow, the bitter weeping of a Simon Peter after denying his Lord.

We also know what a revolution is. It overthrows an old government and installs a new one. So revolutionary repentance is throwing off the old government of selfish desires, sinful actions and satanic influence. Then it installs the new government of Christ's rule. As a result, we do things differently, just as a new government does things in a different way because it is ruled by new and different policies. It has new ideas, new expectations, new policies, new rules, new leaders.

Revolutionary repentance affects how we live, not just what we claim to believe (see Luke 3:7-14). It is a permanent shift from the old to the new, from darkness to light, from the power of Satan to God (see Acts 20:21; 26:17-18). It opens our eyes, softens our hearts, changes our outlooks. When we engage in revolutionary repentance with total trust in Jesus Christ, He transforms us from the inside out.

Revolutionary repentance sometimes pours out with tears and broken humility. We experience James's exhortation: "Come near to God and he will come near to you. Wash your hands, you sinners, and purify your hearts, you double-minded. Grieve, mourn and wail. Change your laughter to mourning and your joy to gloom. Humble yourselves before the Lord, and he will lift you up" (Jas. 4:8-10). Indeed, as Paul said, "Godly sorrow brings repentance . . . and leaves no regret"(2 Cor. 7:10).

When we are in conflict, and honestly believe we are in the right, our soul-searching must often be more specific. If we grant that 95 percent of the fault lies with the other party, then we still need to look within our own hearts and minds for the 5 percent that is ours. Who, for example, does not struggle with a sense of self-righteousness and even pride when the heat is on? (*We're right and they're wrong!*) Pride is so subtle that if we think we have none, we probably do.

With more subtle sins, the ones harder to discern, it helps to make our confession and repentance specific, like aiming a rifle at a precise target. In our book *Setting Your Church Free,* we describe a four-step "announce-renounce" pattern that has proven helpful to many people.[2] This form of revolutionary repentance is prayed daily for 40 days in a row. As we renew our minds, we alert our senses to any repeat behavior. As soon as this sin or fault or weakness shows up, we say to ourselves, *I can't do that. I've been renouncing that activity. That's not who I am anymore.* Take pride as an example:

- I renounce pride in all its subtle, selfish forms.
- I announce that in Christ I am clothed with His humility.

- I affirm that a haughty spirit goes before a fall (see Prov. 16:18).
- I will clothe myself with humility in practical, others-serving actions.

In times of persistent conflict, revolutionary repentance pinpoints our response to problem-producing personalities. Suppose it is a slow-simmering critic who persistently irritates us, but never causes a big enough threat to create a crisis. A fitting renunciation might go something like this:

- I renounce my crummy attitude and defensiveness toward Vince and his disapproval/criticism of me.
- I announce that in Christ I have love for all those within my realm of influence, including Vince, who criticizes my approach and communicates poorly with me.
- I affirm that Jesus taught us to love one another, lay down our lives for our friends, love our enemies and forgive as we have been forgiven (see Matt. 5:44; 6:14-15; John 13:34; 15:13; Col. 3:13).
- I will forgive Vince, speak well of him and contact him from time to time to see what I can do to serve him or to help him.

Consider another example: Suppose we find ourselves always straightening others out. We serve as the moral police officers, especially of those who see our faults. After awhile we begin to realize that we are coming across as condemning, not edifying; we are tearing down, not building up. Something about getting the plank out of our own eye really helps us see the speck in our brother's eye more clearly (see Matt. 7:1-5). The Lord gets our attention, and we want to repent. But how do we break the negative habit? Pray this for 40 days, and see what happens.

- I renounce condemnation, ways of being negative and condemning of others.
- I announce that in Christ I have the grace that accepts, affirms, cheerleads, rejoices, gives thanks and lifts others in prayer.
- I affirm that there is no condemnation in Christ Jesus (see Rom. 8:1), and so there should be none in me, either.
- I will speak positively to others, about others, and I will stop trying to correct others, especially those closest to me. When confrontation is necessary, I will do it full of grace and with a spirit of restoration.

One final example will drive the point home. Suppose that we want to reconcile with someone at work, home or school. But the other person is not interested. They prefer to put up a good front before others while they quietly ignore us, snub us and give us the cold shoulder. We find this kind of behavior highly irritating, if not maddening! As we search our own hearts, we find nothing we have done wrong—except allowing ourselves to be irritated at being mistreated. So, we renounce our irritability:

- I renounce my irritability.
- I announce that in Christ I have peace and a bridled tongue.
- I affirm that I'm commanded to bear with one another and love one another and let the peace of Christ rule in my heart and be thankful (see John 13:34; Col. 3:13,15).
- I will crucify the irritability of my fleshly nature. Instead, I will laugh more, love more and let irritants go on by. I'll be more fun to live with and less demanding to get my way.

Real and lasting change takes more than saying "I'm sorry." It takes repentance that is revolutionary!

TRUSTING GOD'S SOVEREIGNTY

After the genocide in Rwanda, Africa, in April 1994, missionaries Willard and Doris Ferguson were among the first to return to the country. They served in refugee camps near Goma, Zaire (now the Democratic Republic of Congo) and in Rwanda itself. As a nurse, Doris gave emergency medical aid, and Willard gathered the scattered believers for mutual help and worship. When it was fully safe, they returned to their former home, only to see that it had been totally destroyed with dynamite. All that was left was a pile of bricks and rubble. Heartbreaking!

Five years later, the wreckage was still there, and the Fergusons had an idea. They hired men to move the bricks, dig through the debris and put every piece of paper into cardboard boxes. To their amazement they found all the property rights and important legal papers still in place. They were dirty, but the heap of ruins had protected them from the rain, and those vital legal documents were all intact.

Doris Ferguson mused, "It was so hard to see our house ruined. But if it had been left standing, someone would have moved in right away—and all our vital papers would be gone. In a strange way, God protected us and our future."

Even in situations of conflict and despair, God is sovereignly working out His will. The Holy Spirit is our counselor, our advocate before God and man. He gives unity in the Body of Christ—divine help for mending broken relationships—and we are commanded to try hard to maintain it. "As a prisoner of the Lord, then, I urge you to live a life worthy of the calling you have received. Be completely humble and gentle; be patient, bearing with one another in love. Make every effort to keep the unity of the Spirit through the bond of peace" (Eph. 4:1-3).

When two Christians sharply disagree, both may claim to know the Lord's will in the matter. Each may interpret the same Scripture passages personally, claiming the illumination of the Holy Spirit. Each may say, "The Lord told me." Each may believe that any advantage during the conflict is a direct answer to prayer. In the midst of this confusion it is sometimes best to suspend judgment and listen hard to what other people are saying, especially about our own part in the conflict. In his down-to-earth, insightful book *Well-Intentioned Dragons: Ministering to Problem People in the Church*, Marshall Shelley writes a wonderful chapter entitled "When the Dragon May Be Right." In it, he recounts the old adage: "When one calls you a donkey, ignore him. If two call you a donkey, check for hoof prints. If three call you a donkey, get a saddle."[3]

Sometimes the pain of conflict is so severe that the immediate role of the Holy Spirit seems invisible to us. Well-meaning Christians ask, "What lesson am I supposed to be learning through this?" What they really mean is, "Let's get to the point, God, so we can stop the pain." But some lessons, such as perseverance, require prolonged periods of pain and stress. Enduring the pain is the lesson!

Often the best insights come months or even years after the conflict is over. In reflection, and through added maturity, we see our own poor decision making, inept people skills or faulty communication.

A group of mission-agency executives were sharing stories about their lives and ministries with one another. Some of the most experienced recalled their former mistakes with a sigh and a sense of regret. They knew that God is sovereign and never expected themselves to be perfect, but in light of what had happened, how they wished they could go back and make those decisions over again. We should all learn by our mistakes, especially those that cause other people to suffer.

At the front end of a conflict, we can't play Monday-morning quarterback. We need to engage all the resources God gives, and avoid merely reacting from our gut. One of the greatest resources for every Christian is prayer. The good news is that everyone prays during a conflict. Pain is one of the principal ways that God gets our attention. The bad news is that many do not pray for the right things. They pray about the situation, they pray for relief, they may pray their adversaries will somehow get out of their lives. But seldom do they pray for the Lord to bless their enemies.

If the conflict involves child abuse, adultery, embezzlement, betrayal or terrorism, how do we pray blessing on our enemies? It is not easy, but some prayers are always appropriate. We can pray for repentant hearts on their part. We can pray that they will come to their senses like the prodigal son. We can pray for full reconciliation—with God and with ourselves. We can picture them as already right with God, and pray with that image in our minds for their blessing. If they make no profession of knowing Christ, we can pray for their salvation. When we simply do not know how to pray, we can claim God's promise:

> In the same way, the Spirit helps us in our weakness. We do not know what we ought to pray for, but the Spirit himself intercedes for us with groans that words cannot express. And he who searches our hearts knows the mind of the Spirit, because the Spirit intercedes for the saints in accordance with God's will. And we know that in all things God works for the good of those who love him, who have been called according to his purpose (Rom. 8:26-28).

DAILY PRAYER IN TIMES OF CONFLICT

Jesus taught us to love our enemies and pray for them (see Luke 6:27-36). When we are in the heat of battle, it seems unthinkable that we might want to bless our enemies, but a daily prayer during a time of conflict might help (see Appendix 1 for more prayers).

Holy, holy, holy, Lord God Almighty,
I worship and adore You for who You are and for Your awe-
some greatness. You are the creator of heaven and Earth and
all that is in it. You are the Alpha and Omega, the Beginning
and the End. You are omnipotent, omnipresent, omniscient.
You are the high and holy One who also revives the humble and
contrite heart. I humbly bow before You as my sovereign Lord
and gracious Savior.

You sent Jesus Christ, Your one and only Son, to die on the cross
for me and for my sins. You sent Jesus to reveal Yourself, to
teach me about the government of God (Your kingdom) and to
show me how to live and work in Christ by praying, resolving
conflict and doing my part to bring about reconciliation. Help
me to live by Your kingdom principles. Forgive my trespasses as
I forgive those who trespass against me.

By Your Suffering Servant, Jesus, You bore our sins, sorrows
and weaknesses at the cost of agony and unimaginable suffering.
You took the worst possible pain upon Yourself—both physically
and spiritually. You suffered in terrible anguish, intensified by
insulting rejection. Through this torment and agony You took
our sins, our iniquities, our infirmities, our sorrows upon
Yourself—even though we deserved none of Your sacrificial love.
Help me to identify with Your suffering.

You raised our Lord Jesus from the dead and gave Him the
place of Head of His Body, and Head over all the spiritual and
governmental powers in the universe. He now brings about the

good pleasure of God, the will of God, leading the cause of God the Father throughout the earth. Bring me through this agony to an enjoyment of Your resurrection power.

You alone are worthy of my praise and honor and glory and wealth and wisdom and strength. Everything that I value, including my God-given sense of dignity and worth, I lay before You as my Lord and God, Creator and Redeemer, my sovereign and coming King. I tear down the idols in my heart, anything and everything that takes Your place as a primary source of satisfaction or control. I love You with all my passion and obedience.

In amazement and awe, with trembling, I claim my union with You (provided by our Lord Jesus Christ) as Your child, as Your servant, as Your disciple. I praise You for this privilege of living in Christ. Remind me of my true identity as I go through the pain of this conflict. Somehow bring glory to Yourself by my finishing the work You have given me to do, and by my honoring You with my life and my lips—even when I'm tempted to say things that displease You. Love others through me, especially those who give me such a hard time.

You are the God who acts, the incarnate Christ, the victor over sin and death who holds the keys of Hades. You conquered Satan and all his forces and made a public spectacle of them, triumphing over them through the Cross. Give the evil one no place, no foothold, no stronghold in my life.

You are the God who answers prayer, who sets people free from bondage, who restores the broken and brings home the wanderer. You are the Lord Jesus Christ, who acts with compassion on behalf of the harassed and helpless, the oppressed and the disen-

franchised, the hurting and heartbroken. You are the one who opens blind eyes, who removes defense mechanisms and self-justification, who brings about revolutionary repentance and saving faith. You are the one who heals the brokenhearted and binds up their wounds. Do all of these things for me and also for those who oppose me in this conflict.

Lord, protect me, especially now. You are my refuge, shelter, hiding place, dwelling place, stronghold. I come under the shadow of Your wings. You are my rock, my sword, my shield, my strong tower, my mighty fortress. You are my stability, my weapon, my defense, my security, my protection. I joyfully welcome this God-given union with divine resources—God's Holy Spirit, God's written Word, God's mighty works, God's faithful people.

Thank You for the inheritance that You have given to me—Your salvation, life and kingdom. Thank You for Your promises, blessings, likeness, fullness. Thank You that my inheritance includes the Holy Spirit now and a resurrection body when our Lord Jesus Christ returns. Keep these riches before my mind's eye when I'm tempted to focus only on the pain of this conflict and what to do about it.

For all of this, I praise You and glorify Your name!

In the authority of the Lord Jesus Christ I pray, amen.

CHAPTER 10

WHEN IT'S TIME TO CONFRONT

Talk to the right person in the right spirit. The right person is the one you have the problem with. The right spirit is a learner's heart.

C. W. Perry

Sue was seriously dating Ken, a non-Christian, when Ruth and Gigi found out about it (adapted from a true story, but the names have been changed). The phone call came, and it was Gigi: "Would you be willing to go to lunch with Ruth and me?"

In the course of the phone conversation, it gently came out that since both Ruth and Gigi were Christians married to non-Christians, they wanted to get together. Maybe, just maybe, Sue ought to hear about what life might be like if she married Ken.

Reluctantly, Sue agreed. After all, they went to the same church, and they seemed so kind and concerned. But she was not about to break up with Ken!

The lunch was unforgettable. Two married women and one single woman talking about men might not be that unusual, except they were talking about what it is like for a Christian to live with a non-Christian. Ruth was firm, Gigi compassionate, but both women told their heart-wrenching stories. They shared about conflicts over lifestyle, church, entertainment, children and, ultimately, Christ Jesus Himself. Both women loved their husbands and had no plans to leave them, but the pain they felt was deep, real and, at times, severe. They counseled Sue not to violate Scripture by being unequally yoked to an unbeliever but to marry a man who shared her love for Christ (see 2 Cor. 6:14).

Sue left shaken, wondering, praying. In time, determining that Ken was not sincerely interested in Christ, church and a committed Christian lifestyle, she broke up with him. It hurt at first, but later she was so grateful.

A LIFE-GIVING REBUKE

Sometimes we *need* to hear what we really do *not want* to hear. We want approval, but sometimes we need to hear disapproval. Right then we need chiding, a helpful kind of reprimand. King Solomon, known worldwide for his wisdom, wrote, "He who listens to a life-giving rebuke will be at home among the wise" (Prov. 15:31).

A rebuke is a holy scolding. It is a wise word of correction from someone who knows a better way. It is a wake-up call from a friend who sees what we do not, or will not, see. It is sound counsel when we are going the wrong direction. It is accountability when we are violating God's truths. It is a tug on our leash when we wander from God's paths.

> **THE PERSON WHO LISTENS TO SOUND COUNSEL, AND TESTS IT BY THE SCRIPTURES AND BY OTHER DISCERNING PEOPLE, IS WISE INDEED.**

Wise people sometimes make foolish choices. When they do, someone needs to step forward and say, "There's a better way. The road you are following is not the path of life. You need to make a change, and you need to make it now. Here's my recommendation. Feel free to bounce my ideas off of two or three other Christian people whom you know and respect."

The person who listens to sound counsel, and tests it by the Scriptures and by other discerning people, is wise indeed. Those who change their ways grow in knowledge, understanding and discernment (see Prov. 1:23; 15:32; 17:10; 25:11-12).

A life-giving reprimand is not only helpful, it is essential. We so easily fall short of perfect judgment. We so easily stray away from God's best. We are so easily deceived, sometimes self-deceived. We so easily misunderstand our own motives. We so easily let our feelings cloud sound judgment.

Most of us will welcome life-giving censure if we have already entered into an accountable relationship with a close friend. We may despise it when it comes uninvited from a spouse or an adolescent in our own home. We may like it in public from the pulpit and hate it in private from the pastor. We may enjoy it when it is directed toward someone else and resent it when the target is ourselves.

Proverbs goes on to say, "He who ignores discipline despises himself, but whoever heeds correction gains understanding" (Prov. 15:32). It is in our self-interest to listen intently when someone corrects us. If that word of disapproval is life-giving, then act on it at once. A life-giving rebuke may be just what we need. A holy scolding can save us from making serious mistakes. It is worth listening to, and sometimes it is worth giving to someone else. It may be what someone we love must hear. The Spirit-directed Christian knows not only when to receive a life-giving rebuke, but also when to give one.

By means of a heartfelt discussion, Ruth and Gigi saved Sue from untold heartache. They approached her gently but firmly, just as the Bible teaches: "If someone is caught in a sin, you who are spiritual should restore [her] gently" (Gal. 6:1). Discussion is only one way to bring Christ's peace. Ken Sande, in his book *The*

Peacemaker, shares six constructive ways and six destructive ways that people typically respond to conflict.[1] His slippery slope is well worth reprinting here.[2]

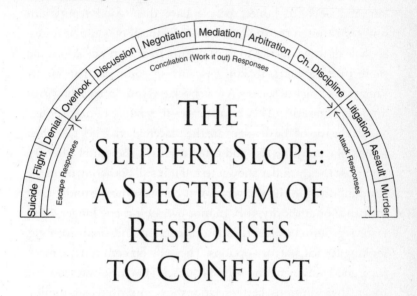

THE SLIPPERY SLOPE: A SPECTRUM OF RESPONSES TO CONFLICT

On the left side of the slippery slope are the escapists—the quitters, the runaways, the milquetoasts, the give-up and give-in types, the ostrich-head-in-the-sand-it's-none-of-my-business-shut-up-and-get-back-to-work types. When there is trouble brewing, they shrug and look the other way. They sigh and lose heart and become disillusioned. At work they become less productive and live for the weekends. At church they move to the fringes of inactivity. At home they act like the proverbial couch potatoes, workaholics or recreation/activity hounds. A few are deeply troubled and shock everyone by committing suicide. These all seem like "nice people" because they avoid trouble. They fake peace—they do not make peace.

On the right side of the diagram are the attackers. Some use anger as their weapon—they are fighters, intimidators, bullies. These people turn red in the face, throw fits, blow up, yell, rage or scream. They often get their way, at least temporarily, but run roughshod over relationships in the process. Some use verbal weapons—gossip, slander, accusations. They undermine, manipulate and lie until honest people have their good reputations dragged through the mud. Some use financial pressure or unreasonable or illegal tactics to force getting their own way. More and more rush to court, making lawsuits so common that we are known as a litigious society. A few shock everyone by engaging in or arranging homicide. They break peace—they refuse to make peace.

At the top of the diagram are the peacemakers. They take their lumps like everyone else and often overlook the minor offenses. Some use the third-day shower test. If it is still bothering them the third morning in the shower, or if it harms someone under their influence or authority, they cannot overlook it any longer. Most resolve group conflicts through discussion and brainstorming, looking for satisfactory options. They rely on committees, meetings, good judgment and sound counsel. They are always looking for creative solutions, better relationships, improved communication. These people know how to negotiate in ways that everyone finds agreement and no one feels taken to the cleaners.

When times of intense, irresolvable conflict come, they rely on company policy, human resource personnel or outside mediators. In churches they look to the pastors and elders, or denominational officials or specialized interventionists. They rely on church polity or established procedures. In the process they work hard to keep their own spirits right, pray for their opponents, try to learn something helpful and live for God's glory. They feel compassion for the peace-fakers who run and feel concern for the peace-breakers who fight. Peace-fakers, peacemakers and peace-breakers will all exist in any group conflict. (A helpful suggestion for those in positions of leadership—moving the peacemakers into positions of influence and authority may be one of the smartest moves in any organization, business or church).

When it comes to personal issues of conflict, peace-fakers and peace-breakers use the same tactics as in a group. So, too, do the peacemakers except that they become much more private, prayerful and concerned about their opponent's reputation and God's glory. Peacemakers hold quiet, often very private, conversations with the other person in the conflict. It is face-to-face, eyeball-to-eyeball, listening, explaining, exploring, trying to understand and work something out. In the most serious cases, they much prefer mediation, arbitration or even church discipline over going to court.

Peacemakers are willing to confront, although usually they do not like to. Peacemakers not only do it, they get good at it. But they know that loving confrontation is most difficult when trying to reconcile people with a close relationship. It may be in the family, in church, at work or at school. The closer the relationship, the greater the pain of conflict.

CONFRONTING PETER IN LOVE

Jesus is the best example of everything. As we look at His confrontations with the 12 disciples, we find that he was tactful, but honest. Jesus did not sidestep issues, but he also protected the other person in the process. He often addressed the Twelve as a group if they were not learning well enough. If the offenses were personal against Himself, He spoke directly to the person.

His words and actions fit the situation perfectly. Compare the differing ways Jesus confronted Simon Peter and Judas Iscariot. Peter made a public claim of being better than the other disciples and insisted that he would die before denying his Lord (see Mark 14:29-31). Jesus responded by openly predicting that Peter would deny Him not once but three times! His life-giving rebuke not only silenced Peter at the moment but later also humbled him for the rest of his life (see Mark 14:66-72; John 21:15-22).

After the Resurrection, after Peter's deep sorrow and repentance, Jesus again confronted him about the denial. Jesus engaged in an interesting tactic. He cooked breakfast for the disciples.

From the disciples' point of view it had been a long night. Hard work, no results and physical fatigue were all they had to show for it. These fishermen felt exhausted. Stress had taken its toll on these men. Their adrenaline had pumped hot and heavy the last few weeks—betrayal, arrest, crucifixion, entombment, marvelous resurrection and surprise appearances. Some physical labor—and making a few bucks as commercial fishermen— would do them good. Or so they thought (see John 21:1-14).

Calling out from the shore, Jesus yelled across 100 yards of water, "Friends, haven't you any fish?" (v. 5). It was the old fisherman's question, "Catch anything?" When the fish are not biting—or, more precisely, are nowhere to be found—a one-word answer will do: "No."

Suddenly the Servant-Leader gave helpful instructions, "Throw your net on the right side of the boat and you will find some" (v. 6). It was a prediction, a prophecy, with up-close verification at hand. They tested it and were unable to haul in the net because of the 153 large fish.

Peter swam or waded to shore to see the risen Lord while the others brought the boat, pulling the net crammed with fish. Next surprise: Somehow Jesus had food cooked and ready— including fish and toast. The Master asked them to add some of their fish, and then He served them breakfast.

As usual, Jesus had something more in mind. He wanted a loving confrontation with Simon Peter about his denial. Three probing, painful questions matched the three times Peter had denied his Lord.

Peter pledged his love again—and Jesus gave him a new job assignment as shepherd instead of fisherman (see John 21:15-23). The risen Lord predicted Peter's painful death and rejected Peter's cry for fairness. Even forgiven sin has its consequences. From then on Peter was faithful to Jesus and became a servant-leader himself, a skilled shepherd of the Lord's flock. He learned to serve, and to confront, for Christ. We can learn too.

Just when we need it, Jesus meets our deepest needs. He cooked breakfast. Just when we feel satisfied, Jesus confronts us with our sin. He searches our hearts. Just when we repent, Jesus restores our dignity. He has something important for us to do. Just when we think everything is okay again, Jesus predicts the consequences of our disobedience. He never lets us off easy. Just when we try to squirm out of something, Jesus reassures us that He is worth anything. He says, "Follow me."

CONFRONTING JUDAS IN LOVE

While Peter's denial was public, Judas Iscariot's soon betrayal was still a secret. So Jesus appealed to him secretly. He confronted in language and actions that Judas understood perfectly, but the other 11 disciples did not. Jesus' first invitation to reconciliation came when the Lord predicted that one of the disciples would betray Him. Judas knew that Jesus was talking about Him, but said nothing. He bypassed the opportunity to confess that he was the one (see John 13:18-21). Instead, the traitor joined the others in denial saying, "Surely not I, Rabbi?" (Matt. 26:25).

A second and more specific opportunity came when Jesus answered Judas' denial, "Yes, it is you" (v. 25). This appears to have been a quiet personal remark to Judas, an appeal for him privately to tell Jesus that he would return loyalty to His Lord. I picture the eyes of Judas dropping to the floor as he turns away from Jesus and starts talking with some other disciple.

The third appeal was acted out, not spoken. During the Last Supper Jesus offered Judas the piece of bread dipped in wine. Everyone recognized that this was a sign of extraordinary friendship and honor. (Can you imagine showing such love to someone who was about to betray you to your death?) Judas Iscariot knew full well that Jesus was communicating that He still loved him and wanted to reconcile. No response. Judas flat-out rejected both the love and the acted-out appeal to reconcile.

When it was certain that Judas Iscariot's course of action was unchangeable, Jesus said, "What you are about to do, do quickly" (John 13:27). Again Judas understood what the Lord meant, although none of the others did. As soon as Judas took the bread, peace-faking as the closest of the Lord's friends, "Satan entered into him" (v. 27). Jesus protected his adversary's dignity, even at their last encounter before betrayal. What an example of working for reconciliation, and accepting the worst consequences when it failed!

> **JESUS IS A PERFECT EXAMPLE OF CONFRONTING IN LOVE.**

If we learn anything from Jesus about confrontation, it is that honest communication is better than devious means of coercion or manipulation. In every case those our Lord confronted heard the charges in ways they could not miss. Jesus is a perfect example of confronting in love. He never resorted to gossip, never took anyone to court, never tried to get even, never stooped to sin. He stood up for the truth, exposed hypocrisy, coached his followers, dealt with problems, spoke the truth in love. He confronted with tact, sensitivity and honesty, and sometimes with astonishing boldness (see Matt. 22).

None of us handles confrontation better than Jesus did, but we can learn from the Master:

- Treat the other person with respect.
- Make the appeal as public or private as the other has set the stage for.
- Take the role of suffering servant rather than self-defender.

WHEN NOT TO CONFRONT

Sooner or later everyone needs to reconcile or help someone else do so. How can we get ourselves ready? It takes courage to confront. It takes humility to lay down our pride and face our own faults. Most people hate confrontation, but everyone loves making up. The fact is that the two go together.

Our friend Norm Whan leads a wonderful ministry called Canning Hunger. He encourages God's people to provide food boxes and canned goods to various agencies that distribute them to hungry children and their families. In December of 2001, Norm was speaking on three consecutive nights at Women's Christmas Tea gatherings for his home church. His goal was to motivate them into positive action for the hungry in their own county. The groups agreed in advance to take an offering for Christmas baskets to feed the disadvantaged.

On the first night, describing the plight of the underprivileged, Norm used the word "rape" and admittedly had a bit of an edge in his voice during his impassioned appeal. Afterward, one woman objected as she handed him the checks from her table. But Norm reasoned to himself that the offering was far more generous than he expected—the emotional jarring may have done some good.

However, later in the week, a good friend phoned. "Norm, you are one of my heroes. I really respect what you are doing," he said. Norm knew something unpleasant was coming next! Gently but firmly his friend let him know that he and his wife felt Norm's comments were out of place. "It would have been fine in a Sunday School lesson or a sermon but not for first-time guests at a Women's Christmas Tea."

Who likes criticism? Since the financial response for the hungry had been so generous the first night, Norm found it hard to take. What should he do? He did not want to change the emotional appeal and watch the offering drop when the poor needed it so desperately. In fact, he had already promised far more boxes than Canning Hunger had the funds to deliver. So he prayed and asked the Lord for acceptable words and for just as much money as the first night. What is more, he asked his confronting friend to come pray with him just before the event!

His friend agreed. After they prayed together and just before Norm walked in to speak, his friend said something Norm will never forget, "Thanks for agreeing to tone down your message. Whatever is given in the offering for the hungry tonight, my wife and I will match!" Norm changed the offensive words and softened his spirit but kept the emotion strong. The offering was slightly more than the first night—and on top of that his friend matched it to the dollar! That man understood loving confrontation!

It takes wisdom to know when to take action and when to let it go. We need to discern whether to speak up or shut up. If it is minor, if it will pass on its own, if it is a personal difficulty or offense, the wise will ignore it. "A man's wisdom gives him patience; it is to his glory to overlook an offense" (Prov. 19:11).

PREPARING TO CONFRONT

When the problem will not go away, when it is grievous, when it just keeps getting worse, then it is time to confront. It helps to prepare in advance. Think through some opening questions or approaches to the other person:

- "Could we talk?"
- "Is this a good time?"
- "How about lunch?"
- "Something's been bothering me. May I share it with you?"
- "Obviously, something is wrong between us. Can you share what you are feeling?"

With some opening questions on the tip of your tongue, talk with the *right person* in the *right spirit* at the *right time* (see Matt. 18:15-17). This seems obvious, but it is amazing how many talk *about* others instead of *to* them. Experience shows that the overwhelming majority of conflicts will work out if we will talk directly to the person involved. It does take a right spirit—a tender heart and a willingness to make up. Always, always, always, timing is important.

Early in the conversation, do something to defuse the tension. The tone of voice communicates even more than the words. "A gentle answer turns away wrath, but a harsh word stirs up anger" (Prov. 15:1). Here are some examples:

- "I've come to realize that I was wrong in . . ." (Never say, "I'm sorry, *but* . . . " Avoid "if" and "maybe.")
- "I need to understand your viewpoint, where you are coming from."
- "I want to be fair. I'm really trying not to blow it."

Use the sandwich method—affirm, confront, affirm. Begin by affirming good things about the other person. Everyone has strengths, so point them out:

- "I respect you for . . ."
- "I admire the way you . . ."
- "I love you because . . ."

When it is time to confront, attack the issue not the person. After listening, after trying to understand, after getting at the heart of the issue, then it is your turn to speak up. Confront the weakness, the fault, the grievance. Speak the truth in love. Jesus taught, "Show him his fault, just between the two of you" (Matt. 18:15). Remember the velvet-covered brick—honesty wrapped in love can get the attention of even a thick skull. Consider these statements:

- "If I share with you how I feel, will you promise not to get angry (withdraw, clam up or have any expected negative response)?"
- "What's really hurting me is . . ."
- "We just can't go on like this. We must set some boundaries."

At the close of the conversation, return to affirming again:

- "Thank you for talking with me about this."
- "I really appreciate your openness. It must have been difficult for you to be so honest with me."
- "May I pray a blessing on you?"

Since every person and every situation is unique, conflict is always complex. A one-size-fits-all solution never exists. A few guidelines, however, can make a big difference.

Try Your Best and Ask the Other Person to Try
If one person tries to reconcile, something can happen. If both people try, much will happen. If nobody tries, nothing will happen. Be the one who is willing to try to reconcile.

Lay Down Your Pride
God rewards humility by pouring His grace over it (see Prov. 3:34;

Jas. 4:6-10; 1 Pet. 5:5-6). No one thinks, *I'm proud*; instead they think, *It's the principle of the thing*, or *I don't deserve to be treated this way*. Pride always says, "It's your fault. You're wrong." Pride refuses to say, "I'm wrong." If you think you are pride-free, in the middle of a conflict try speaking the nine hardest words in the English language, "I was wrong. You were right. Please forgive me." Stan Leach, current superintendent of Evangelical Friends Church Southwest, says that if you repeat it until it sounds canned, then try adding one line, "I was wrong. You were right. Please forgive me. I'm a jerk!"

Listen to Learn

A wise old saying directs, "Seek to understand before you seek to be understood." Listen to the opponent, listen intently, and then listen some more. Ask yourself, "What's the grain of truth in the criticism or the valid point of the gripe? What can I learn here?" When the other person has said it all, ask another probing question, "What else are you feeling?" Then listen some more. Then ask, "Is anything else bothering you?"

Look for the Highest and Best Motives

"You really want our office to become a better workplace, don't you?" "Oh, I see, what you really want is for our marriage to get better and better." "I'm beginning to understand that our friendship is really important to you." This is the godly opposite of assigning the worst motives to your adversary.

Forgive and Keep on Forgiving

We cannot repeat this principle too often. Resentment and bitterness work like infection in a wound. Forgiveness cleans it out. Forgiveness gives freedom, release, relief. Jesus taught that it was essential if we want our own sins forgiven (see Matt. 6:14-15).

Resolve the Tangible Issues

Money, custody, property, workmanship, alimony—whatever the concrete problems, work them out. Negotiate. Compromise. Go the extra mile. Do whatever it takes to resolve the material issues.

Grow in Wisdom

Reconciling with someone will not prevent all future conflicts. But each reconciliation can make us wiser, smarter and kinder. We learn what to do, and not do, the next time.

WILL CONFRONTATION WORK WITH A JERK?

What if the other person has a problem-producing personality? Then what? Loving approaches that work well with normal, healthy people often do not work with these types. So what do we do? The book of Proverbs calls this kind of person a "fool" and makes it clear that no single approach will always work. For example, two back-to-back Proverbs purposely give opposite counsel: "Do not answer a fool according to his folly, or you will be like him yourself" (26:4) and "Answer a fool according to his folly, or he will be wise in his own eyes" (26:5).

Wisdom teaches us to respond one way in certain circumstances and another way on different occasions. Sometimes it is smart to say nothing, or to give a discreet answer. At other times it is smarter to humor someone, or even use some well-chosen humorous nonsense to let the person know that he or she is not so smart after all.

Sometimes it takes a lot of suffering, as shown in this true story (the names and places have been changed). For eight years Ross Bishop faced workplace harassment. His immediate supervisor, Peter Harrison, was from the old school of hard-boiled factory bosses. He saw himself as the tough guy, the ruler, the big boss. Actually he was not the big boss at all, just a department head in a large utility in New York. Intimidation, aggravation and manipulation were stock-in-trade with Peter, and Ross bore the brunt of it.

Ross was a Christian, although he seldom spoke of his faith at work. Yet everyone knew. Peter despised goody-goodies and made Ross his special target. He was always on his back, always goading him, never satisfied. Around the other employees, the verbal and emotional abuse were unrelenting. The strange thing about Peter was that when he was alone with Ross, he was super nice to him. But in the presence of other employees he made things rough.

The boss above Peter would ask Ross to go get something on the other side of the yard. When he started to walk across the yard, Peter would yell, "Where are you going?"

"To get the equipment that the boss asked me to."

"Go back to your desk. I'm your boss. He's not!"

Then the other boss would come around and say, "Did you get that equipment?"

"No, Peter said not to."

So Ross was always caught between two bosses, and yet Peter's superiors did not discipline him. They thought he ran a tight ship and made them money, so they looked the other direction. Worse yet, they feared his intimidation. Peter loved to bypass his immediate boss and go to management. For some unknown reason, his immediate boss did not have the guts or the political clout to do anything about Peter's unacceptable behavior.

Joseph (see Genesis 37–50) was Ross's inspiration, and he consciously tried to follow Joseph's example. He thought about changing jobs or asking for a transfer to another department, but the nudging from the Holy Spirit was always the same: *No, not now, not yet.* So he waited.

During this time of waiting, Ross learned a lot about refusing to carry resentment. He forgave Peter—and kept on forgiving him—not allowing bitterness to dig roots into his heart. He learned to unload his anger every day. True, the pain of constant aggravation wounded him, but the absence of bitterness caused the wounds to heal well.

After eight years and no change in Peter's tyrannical behavior, Ross did apply for a job as a buyer within the same company. Because of his positive attitude, he was selected for the job.

Some time later, Peter's boss received the shocking diagnosis of cancer and soon retired. It was time for a change. Because of all the personnel problems in the department, management decided to phase out the group entirely but wanted someone to move back in for the transition. Who did they tap but Ross Bishop?

At first, Ross said no, but they asked again. So he countered with three conditions.

1. Everyone in authority above him would back up his decisions—including firing any employees who caused problems.
2. No one in supervision was to tolerate any employee's trying to go around him. If Peter tried, they would come to Ross to work out the issue.
3. He would take the job for only two months. (He actually served as department manager for 20 years).

After discussion, management agreed, and suddenly Ross was Peter's boss. Peter Harrison felt terror all the way to his bones. The man he had persecuted now had power over him. What Proverbs predicted had come true, "The fool will be servant to the wise" (Prov. 11:29). But like Joseph, Ross treated Peter kindly but fairly. No more long lunches, no more special privileges—but no retaliation. Ross tried not to make life miserable for his former tormenter.

Peter could not handle it. He might have endured harassment but to be killed with kindness was too much. After three months he retired. That is not the end of the story. Several times he came back to visit his old cronies, but then he showed a totally different attitude. He brought Ross home-grown cherries! He treated him with respect, even kindness.

Years later another young man in the company was facing a similar kind of harassment. Other employees told him about Ross, who was almost a legend by then, and sent him in to talk to Ross. He was not the only one; several managers sought out Ross for counsel. Ross's forgiveness and endurance paid long-term dividends in respect and in future opportunities.

CARRYING PAIN

Many people today are carrying pain that did not originate with them. It is sad, because so often it is unnecessary. Want to unload? Release the burden? Let someone else carry the freight? Ask yourself a simple question: As a Christian, is this pain assigned to me by Christ? Or is this hurt something He died to remove? Ask it another way: Is this cross I carry a consequence of being a Christian and as such assigned by God? Or is it the result of someone else's abuse or neglect and as such should be carried by Christ? Or is it from my own sin that is in need of forgiveness and cleansing? (If so, I can rightly make an appeal to God to remove at least some of the consequences.)

What a big difference between carrying my cross and carrying unnecessary pain. My cross is a willingness to die for Jesus, suffer for Him, live for Him no matter what the cost. He commands me to carry it (see Luke 9:23-25). But my load of pain is something He wants to carry for me. It is a great trade. I give

Him my cares, and He gives me His cross (see Matt. 10:38). I give Him my weary load, and He gives me His strength (see Isa. 40:28-31). I give Him my pain, and He gives me His yoke (see Matt. 11:28-30). I give Him what is killing me, and He gives me something worth dying for (see Matt. 10:39).

Jesus Christ comes along with a big truck. He offers you a ride. You accept and climb into the cab with your heavy backpack still on. With a smile, the Lord invites you to take off the backpack and throw it onto the bed of His truck. He assures you that His truck is big enough to carry you and your load with no strain at all. Ask Him. Ask Him to take your anxieties, guilt, burdens—especially the pain that came from parents, spouses or anyone else who has hurt you. One more thing: The way that you unload is by forgiving those who loaded you up (see Matt 18:15-35).

CHAPTER 11

WHEN YOU NEED A GOOD PROCESS

Can good friendships die? They can. But don't let them go hastily or in anger; friendships are too hard to come by, too precious.
Ray and Anne Ortlund, *A Fresh Start for Your Friendships*

More than 20 years ago, Collin and Tiffany (from a Muslim nation, names have been changed) were the best of friends as they served in an effective youth ministry. Many of their peers found Jesus Christ as their Lord and Savior, and with their group of friends they enjoyed fun, fellowship and fruitfulness. It was an exhilarating adventure. Their Christian friendship never turned to romance, and they each married someone else, establishing their own families. Their paths continued in similar ministries through the years. Collin went to Bible college, and Tiffany attended seminary and became a gifted teacher and leader. Now some 20 years later, Collin was the government-registered leader of a small Christian denomination, and Tiffany had become influential in the same denomination where Collin was the executive. That's when the trouble began.

At first it was simple disagreement about money issues and administrative decisions, but then it became more personal. Tiffany and her husband had the courage to speak out against what they saw as an abuse of power. Collin sensed their disloyalty toward him personally, but he denied that any major problem existed. When Tiffany and her husband were ready to go on a new missions trip, the funds Collin controlled were somehow extremely limited for their ministry. Yet similar ministries seemed to get funded without a problem. Tiffany was angry and hurt; Collin was reserved but refused to budge on most of the final decisions. Each saw the other as someone who had become contentious and self-centered. This division at the highest levels of the church was evident to everyone around them.

The two took the first step toward reconciliation by talking in ways that were culturally appropriate, but no resolution came. Frustration mounted on both sides, but no reconciliation was in sight. At this point, a missionary and a foreign denominational leader began a peacemaking process. It was time for the second step toward reconciliation.

Our Lord told us to "go and be reconciled to your brother" (Matt. 5:24). Nothing in this passage limits it to one visit. In fact, in Matthew 18:16 our Lord instructs us to "take one or two others along" to meet with the offender a second time. The suggested process that follows combines the teaching of these two passages with special focus on the role of the antagonists and the one or two others.

Speaking of contentious people in the church, Marshall Shelley says, "The spirit needed for confronting dragons is not one of fear and withdrawal nor of arrogant power. It is gentleness and firmness—an attitude of smart love."[1] "Smart love"— what a fine phrase to describe what is needed. When the one-on-one loving confrontation discussed in the last chapter does not resolve the conflict, we're tempted to give up on reconciliation. Many back out of the relationship altogether or continue their fight in court. Instead, we need to use smart love, following Jesus' teaching.

A few antagonists refuse to meet a second time, but many will not. Wisdom says to take along those people whom the other person will respect and trust. Avoid people who will poison the process or who want to destroy the adversary. What is the role of the one or two others? Several functions come to mind.

1. *They verify the facts.* This may be the primary meaning of Jesus' statement that "every matter may be established by the testimony of two or three witnesses" (Matt. 18:16).
2. *They calm the hostility.* People in conflict feel more restrained when every word and action is under observation.
3. *They clarify communication.* When something is unclear, or the two antagonists see the situation so differently, the two or three witnesses ask questions that bring out the facts. Sometimes they confront the antagonists.
4. *They search for possible solutions.* A small group of three or four (the two antagonists and one or two others) can often come up with options that will satisfy both parties. Caution: The one or two should stimulate those directly in conflict to suggest alternatives rather than imposing a settlement.
5. *They provide accountability.* If both antagonists know and respect the one or two others, their agreement is on record with them. It follows that these witnesses have an opportunity to help both hold to their agreements.

Smart love would suggest one more thing—a good process to follow. A process alone will not resolve a conflict, but a good process is far better than a poor one or no process at all. It gives a track to run on that has proved helpful to others. It moves the antagonists from frustration and hostility toward honest discussion and fair resolution. If both know Christ, sometimes full reconciliation will result.

For the purposes of this chapter, assume that both parties are willing to meet and that both are Christians. With a non-Christian, the process might help achieve some peacemaking, but full biblical reconciliation in Christ will not be possible. Christian reconciliation begins with God Himself, so we strongly recommend that the best preparation is to take each of those involved in the conflict through Neil Anderson's *The Steps to Freedom in Christ*.[2] Before the reconciliation meeting, the one or two others who come along should also process the Steps to Freedom. Nothing helps both facilitators and antagonists as much as being fully and completely at peace with God themselves.

> **CHRISTIAN RECONCILIATION BEGINS BY OUR BEING RECONCILED WITH GOD HIMSELF.**

The process used with Collin and Tiffany has been expanded and revised over time but still has the same major components. We now call it The Seven Steps Toward Biblical Reconciliation (for an expanded explanation of these steps, see Appendix 2). Following these guidelines will help people deal with personal, spiritual and material issues. Each person processes the Steps to Reconciliation before God as well as with each other. If two others are present, one will serve as the facilitator and the other as a prayer partner. Each may also coach the reconciling parties in private conferences as needed (see "Tips for the Facilitator and Prayer Partner" located at the end of Appendix 2).

These steps differ somewhat from usual mediation practices in that facing biblical issues such as mutual forgiveness and heart reconciliation is built in to the process itself. The more common mediation approach relies on instruction and the role of a mediator who negotiates the process. The Steps to Reconciliation depend upon the Lord to be the mediator, and one or two mature Christians to facilitate the process (see 1 Tim. 3:1-15; Titus 1:6-9).

THE SEVEN STEPS TOWARD BIBLICAL RECONCILIATION

Step 1: Image of God Versus Sinful Nature

Each person lists the good things—strengths, qualities and character of the other person. Each one states them aloud to the other.

The Bible says we were all created in the image of God (see Gen. 1:27). Although sin tarnished that image, we each retain some character strengths and positive qualities. This step acknowledges who we are in Christ: image-bearers of our creator and redeemed children of God. Everyone has strengths and weaknesses—everyone! This is the time to state the strengths.

In Burundi, a small nation in the heart of Africa, a national leader taught this process to a group of pastors. Everyone was thrilled. They found that the first two steps make deposits in the emotional "love bank" of the other person. Rehearsing positive character qualities (Step 1) and recalling good memories (Step 2) builds up an account in the emotional bank.

The Burundian pastors serve people who have all lost relatives through mistrust, murder and revenge because of horrible conflicts between the Hutu and Tutsi tribes. Yet they found these first two steps as the most remembered and most practical. As their leader put it, "When they reminded each other about the good, it took care of the bad." People in conflict normally focus almost entirely on the problem and demean the other person. It is a pleasant surprise to hear good things about ourselves from the lips of our adversaries. The next two or three steps will require "withdrawals" from that love bank—sometimes painful ones. So the more deposits that can be made here, the better.

Remember Collin and Tiffany in a Muslim country, who were once close, like brother and sister, but are now at odds? Suspicion replaced trust, and both justified their own positions. Before addressing any of the problems in their conflict, Collin and Tiffany each recalled the other's strengths and fine character qualities. Everyone appreciated this step, and the feeling of hostility between them thawed considerably.

Step 2: Good Memories Versus Blanked-Out Memories

Each person rehearses aloud the good memories from their relationship in the past.

Conflict, especially among Christians, often occurs between people who have had a good relationship in the past. It is possible that the antagonists, like Collin and Tiffany, once felt like brothers and sisters in Christ. If it is appropriate, rehearse how they worked together in the cause of Christ, or enjoyed great social times or even grew up as part of the same family. If the relationship is more distant, some experiences of good memories may still be present. Before addressing any of the problems, each one recalls the good memories, and these are recorded by the facilitator or prayer partner.

If those in conflict have a long relationship, it helps to break the memories into segments. What were the best memories in each decade of life—teens, 20s, 30s, 40s? If it is a much shorter time frame, they can begin with when they first came into contact with each other. It is important for the facilitator and prayer partner not only to hear the items each one mentions in Step 1 and Step 2, but also to write them down. Reviewing them at the end, or in tense times during the process, may prove helpful.

Most of Collin and Tiffany's memories were highly positive, especially those of when they were younger. At times they smiled or even laughed as they recounted their experiences. Recalling those memories changed the atmosphere of the session, making it much more positive than when it began. Their emotional love banks had enough deposits that they were ready for the pain that was sure to surface as they discussed their present conflict.

Step 3: Verbalized Pain Versus Hidden Pain

Each person names the failures and painful memories that have damaged their relationship, beginning with their earliest memories. By the end of this step, each one will respond by telling the other, "From your description of what happened, I can now see how I hurt you. I was wrong [or sinned against you] in (specifically name the offense)." Both parties must acknowledge what they have done that hurt the other person and acknowledge their own part in the offense. At the end of this step, *both people pray and confess before God their own part in the conflict.*

Since Adam and Eve fell into sin, all the rest of us have followed in their footsteps (see Gen. 3; Rom. 3:23). No one is perfect. All have sinned. Everyone has flaws, character defects and weaknesses. In any conflict, something happened to trigger the trouble. Often it was a series of events, or a demonstration of a persistent sin or weakness, such as adultery, rage, gossip, criticism or misunderstanding. Sometimes it involved a material issue such as a broken contract, real-estate matter, unpaid loan, child-custody argument, personal injury or landlord/renter dispute. Acknowledging sins, wrongdoings or faults against another person is often a big step toward reconciliation, but first they must be heard from the one who feels wronged.

One of the two people involved in the conflict goes first and shares the painful memory farthest back in time. The second person listens without interruption. When finished with the viewpoint of the sin, abuse, disappointment or emotional pain, the second person can ask for clarification if necessary. Sometimes the facilitator may want to ask the listener to repeat what was said, including the intensity of feeling, so the first person feels heard. Then the second person responds with his or her own account of the same incident.

The first person proceeds to the next memory. It often helps to follow a time line with the oldest painful memories first. After each incident is recalled, the second person rehearses the same memory from a personal point of view.

After listening, each person acknowledges his or her own wrong to the other. First one and then the other says, "From your description of what happened, I can now see how I hurt you. I was wrong [or sinned against you] in (specifically name the offense)." Both parties must acknowledge what they have done to hurt the other person and their responsibility for it.

At the end of this step, *both people pray and confess before God their own part in the conflict.* For Christians, confessing to God is an effective way to clear the air of misunderstanding and unhappiness.

Collin and Tiffany were honest with each other. They spoke respectfully, but they did not hide their disappointment and misgivings. As each one rehearsed a painful memory, the other responded with a personal view of the same incident. It was not enjoyable, but it did clear the air of misunderstanding. Each gained insight from the other. The length of their relationship, going back many years, helped in understanding the depth of hurt. It was beautiful to hear each one pray about personal shortcomings, confessing them to the Lord and before each other. (If one or both refuse to cooperate at this point, simply keep going and return to this step later.)

Step 4: Seeking Forgiveness Versus Claiming Innocence

Each person asks forgiveness of the other, saying aloud, "I was wrong. Will you forgive me for what I did when I (name the hurts, disappointments, wrongs and sins)?" Encourage both parties to ask forgiveness from the other. Lasting reconciliation will seldom come without asking for and receiving forgiveness. It gives each a fresh start, an opportunity to change for the better.

Although it seemed a bit tentative, Collin and Tiffany did speak words of forgiveness. Later events proved they meant it. But this was not the end of the session. More steps were yet to come.

Step 5: Stated Commitments Versus Wishful Thinking

Each person tells the other, "Before the Lord, I am going to do my best to become the person God created me to be. In the spirit of Christian love, I will do or will stop doing the following in regard to our relationship (state specific actions)." If helpful, the other may respond with "It would make it easier for me to follow through on our reconciliation if you would/would not (state a specific desired action)."

Stating specific commitments in a spirit of love clears up expectations. It replaces wishful thinking and hoping for the best. Speaking the truth in love nudges each one from forgiveness toward lasting change. Each person in a conflict needs to hear what the other is willing to do or stop doing.

> **SPEAKING THE TRUTH IN LOVE NUDGES EACH ONE FROM FORGIVENESS TOWARD LASTING CHANGE.**

Collin had received most of the heat from Tiffany up to this point. Now he had his chance to declare his intentions, and he was articulate in what he needed from Tiffany, his chief critic. It would help him if she did not criticize outside the normal decision-making meetings and if she would refrain from speaking about him in a negative way. Tiffany was now a little more reserved. Once she had unloaded her pain, it took a while to think about how she was supposed to relate to Collin and how he could help her carry out her responsibilities.

When material issues are involved, this is the time for brainstorming. Encourage both to come up with possible solutions to their problem. Write these thoughts down, encouraging one idea to stimulate another. Explain that we will evaluate the ideas later and select the best ones. At this point it is off-limits to criticize anything mentioned, no matter how far-fetched or unreasonable it may sound. Gather as many suggestions as possible.

Step 6: Covenant of Agreement Versus Hardened Positions

> The two talk together about what they are willing to agree to. If a material issue is involved, the two discuss possible ways to settle the dispute (you can use the brain-

storming list from the previous step). As they reach agreement on each issue, with the guiding wisdom of the one or two others, they put it into a covenant of agreement before God. Both sign this covenant.

A covenant between adversaries is a biblical and time-honored way of building a lasting peace (see Gen. 31:44). Simply hearing the other person's commitments and desires for change is good. Reaching an agreement and putting it in writing as a covenant is even better. Evaluate the commitments, desires, ideas and solutions mentioned in the last step, looking for the best solutions that both can agree on. Pray in faith for God's wisdom.

After several hours in working through the previous steps, Collin and Tiffany worked out their original problem in less than 30 minutes. Both were happy with the agreement. In their oral culture, it did not seem necessary or even helpful to put the agreement in writing. However, with Americans in conflict we have found that writing out the agreement is a big plus!

If agreement does not come easily, it may well be time for some personal coaching, asking each participant to step outside for a moment. Sometimes one of those in the conflict will share facts or feelings with the facilitator that they will not say face-to-face in the group. The facilitator and prayer partner may need to encourage adoption of one of the better solutions, urge a reasonable compromise or suggest a negotiation strategy. If one person is far more dominant than the other, or in a powerful position of authority, the facilitator must be careful to keep the process fair to both.

Something about writing down the original strengths shared at the beginning of the session and writing the agreement at this point makes the reconciliation easy to review. *Each person should sign the covenant when it is concluded.*

But what happens if no unity exists? What can help?

1. *Recall our resources in Christ.* If we are not in heart unity, then we are confused. The God of unity is not confused because He has only one will. Ask the participants what they believe is God's best in this matter. Seek the Lord in prayer together to reveal His will.

2. *Read the original strengths and good memories shared in Steps 1 and 2.* Ask each one to reaffirm one strength or good memory that seems pertinent to the settlement at this point.

3. *Prayerfully discuss until we reach unity.* It is not unusual to have long discussions and differences of opinion in coming to unity on what God's will is. What is important is that the two are "being of the same mind" (Phil. 2:2, *NASB*) or "being like-minded" (*NIV*), or, literally, in the Greek, "think the same thing." The Greek word has the idea of both thought and feelings, both head and heart. If the facilitator senses no progress in spirit and attitude and sees that one or both of the parties involved simply love to fight, then it is best to close the session. If progress in becoming like-minded is happening, it may be good to take each aside in a private conference and ask, "What will it take to reconcile with your brother or sister in Christ?" or at the very least, "What can we work out here?" It may take *readjusting the expectations,* thinking of God's best for everyone rather than one's own level of satisfaction. It may take *a fresh perspective* on the situation, which the facilitator and prayer partner can bring. It may take *new boundaries,* a no-harm covenant that separates

the two in agreed ways. If one or both cannot go along with a suggested proposal, then this may be the time for the facilitator and prayer partner to suggest a reasonable solution.

4. *Schedule another session a week or so later.* Celebrate any progress made, including in spirit and in attitudes. Encourage each one to keep praying, seeking wise counsel from respected Christians. In the case of material issues, recommend good advice from mutually recognized experts.

5. *Once unity is reached, the participants stand by the decisions agreed on.* If material issues are involved, it may well be best to have the parties' attorneys draw up the final agreement of the items in the covenant of agreement. Accountability to someone, possibly the one or two who have facilitated the settlement, greatly helps. Each person should sign the covenant when it is concluded, and copies should be given to those involved, including those who will hold the two parties accountable.

Step 7: Blessings Versus Resentments

Each person prays blessings, thanksgiving and praise upon the other.

Jesus taught us to love our enemies, do good to those who hate us, pray for those who mistreat us and bless those who curse us (see Luke 6:27-28). What better time to obey Him than at the close of a reconciliation session? This puts Christ's positive touch upon each other and upon the relationship from this point onward. Each person should pray spontaneous blessings on the other.

This step was added after the reconciliation session with Collin and Tiffany. It has proven to be a winner. It is beautiful to behold former adversaries praying God's blessings upon each other. It is biblical, practical and effective!

Conclusion

If the parties reached biblical reconciliation, a sense of relief and praise to God will often seem evident. If they merely reached a negotiated agreement, then thank the Lord for the progress. If they reached no accord, then thank the participants for their efforts. It may be wise to recommend professional mediators or binding arbitration in matters with material issues involved. Valuable Christian mediation services are available.[3]

The list of strengths and good memories from Steps 1 and 2, along with the written covenant from Step 7, should be copied for each participant, including the facilitator and prayer partner.

The facilitator explains that one reconciliation session does not prevent future conflict, as we all know from our own marriage and family relationships. It is important now for each to give the other person permission to speak the truth with love and mutual respect when future conflicts arise.

Leave one another thanking God that He has provided reconciliation through our Lord Jesus Christ.

ANOTHER PROCESS

In rare cases where those in conflict did not know each other previously, another kind of process might be more helpful. Most mediators, both secular and Christian, rely on a modified negotiation strategy. They follow a process that tries to bring the two sides together by discussion, compromise, negotiation and the help of trained mediators.[4] Peacemakers Ministries suggests such a process, based on the acronym GOSPEL.

GOSPEL Mediation Process

Greeting and ground rules: Make introductions and agree on how you will work together.

Opening statements: Ask each party to briefly explain what he or she would like to accomplish.

Storytelling: Help the parties to clearly communicate all relevant information.

Problem identification and clarification: Clearly define central issues and interests.

Explore Solutions: Brainstorm options; evaluate them reasonably and objectively.

Lead to agreement: Encourage and document a final agreement.[5]

WHEN RECONCILIATION DOES NOT WORK

One of life's most frustrating experiences is to try to make up with an adversary who will not reconcile. It may be at home with a family member, at work with a colleague or at church with an offended friend. Rehearse the scenes in your mind. You prayed for wisdom and for God's best for the other person. You tried to forget it, but the hurt was too deep. So you forgave, you released it and turned it all over to God.

Forgiveness always brings fresh freedom in Christ, but the relationship remained strained, uncomfortable, even tense. So you took the next step. You talked with the person, not just once but on several occasions. Tough beans. No dice. Thumbs down. You called for one or two others and went through the Seven Steps Toward Biblical Resolution listed in this chapter. The response to all this effort was also negative—and no hope was given for any reconciliation that was anywhere close to reasonable and fair. Your friends who tried to help agreed that you had gone the second mile. But the other person refused to budge.

Now what? What does a Christian do when an offended brother or sister refuses to reconcile? No pat answers exist, but here are a few starting points.

Work on Yourself

Focus on being the person God called you to be. Do what Christ commands you to do. Obey the written Word of God. Ask the Holy Spirit to help you change for the better. The fastest way to cause a change in someone close to you is to make a personal change. Become the ideal parent, spouse, friend, colleague or brother. Overcome your own shortcomings. Remove your adversary's excuses. Confess your own sins. Maximize your own strengths. Bloom where you are planted.

Pray Daily Blessings for the Other Person and Do Good to This Person

"But I tell you who hear me: Love your enemies, do good to those who hate you, bless those who curse you, pray for those who mistreat you" (Luke 6:27-28). Say a prayer every day, "Lord, bless this person in ways that will lead him (or her) into Your best." Look for an opportunity to do this person a favor. Find ways to show tangible love.

Wait—Give It Time

Be patient as God is patient. How long did He wait for you? How much time did He give you? Did He cut you some slack when He forgave you? The father of the prodigal son in Luke 15 waited until his son came to his senses and then came home. David sang in the book of Psalms, "I waited patiently for the LORD; he turned to me and heard my cry" (Ps. 40:1). Keep pace with God's timing, even if you hate waiting.

Win Allies Around the Offended Person

If the relationship is a relative or someone you want to win back at all costs, look for allies. Who are the closest friends or family members? To whom do they talk? Who will listen to complaints? Begin winning these people over. Pray that God will give you favor in their eyes. Win their friendship, do them a good turn, but do not become a pest or a bother. Do not become manipulative, but do become a blessing. If you cannot make progress with an important person in your life, build positive relationships with their influencers.

Find God's Perspective

What is He up to in all this? Is He preparing you for something better? Teaching you character? Giving you experiences for future greatness? Fulfilling some bigger purpose? Remember, unresolved conflict sent Jesus to the cross, and provided salvation for the world (see Gen. 50:20; Rom. 8:28). It is a myth that we can settle every conflict. But beware of the opposite deception. An unresolved conflict never gives permission to act in a less than Christian way. When reconciliation does not work, become Christlike in conduct. Ask Jesus to turn pain into progress and frustration into fruitfulness.

MELT AN ICEBERG

The best way to melt an iceberg is to keep the sun shining, bright and warm, for a long time. Some people try to melt an iceberg with a hair dryer—a burst of searing heat. Hair dryers may work for ice cubes, but icebergs take more time, more warmth, more sunshine. Here are a few ways to turn up the heat on that frozen relationship. Prepare now for the next time you will meet the one who is chilled out. Pray for grace, and seek out the best counsel on specific steps to take. For example, ask, "Lord, what do You want me to do? How do You want me to act?" Search for His counsel as you might look for the best stock purchase or sale item.

The Holy Spirit may direct you to speak positively about this person to friends or relatives. When you find something to compliment or praise, somehow the word gets back. A pastor of an earlier generation always seemed to attract men to his church. His son, who became a pastor himself, asked his secret. "I see all men as angels," he responded, "and soon they become that way." No matter how brutal your iceberg or how many ships it has sunk, remember that it cannot maintain its cutting edges in the presence of tropical sunshine.

When you meet Mr. Ice or Ms. Frozen, smile and give a warm greeting from your heart. Often we need to thaw out our own hearts with Christ's love and grace. No matter how cold the response, keep the sun shining. Stay friendly. Lower your voice. Make eye contact. Grin. Chuckle. Laugh. If Mrs. Cold throws ice cubes, duck and do not throw any back. If a conversation opens up, pay attention. Ask questions about family, friends, the other person's interests. Take a genuine interest in what the other cares about or is interested in. Pray silently as the icy one talks, even if the conversation is cold or hostile. If the adversary unloads anger, criticism or sarcasm, let it fly by like an arrow that misses its target. When the tirade stops, say something soothing and remain gracious.

Gracious people are well liked, respected and enjoyable to be around. They smile easily and often and sometimes have an engaging sense of humor. They constantly make others feel at ease and relaxed. Think of the finest and best Christians you know. Is it not true that they are gracious people? Consideration and kindness fill their lives and spill from their lips. "Words from a wise man's mouth are gracious, but a fool is consumed by his own lips" (Eccles. 10:12).

Gracious people are sweet spirited. You sense peace in their presence. They are habitually kind, patient and generous. A gracious spirit shines through them with a beauty greater than any diamond.

How did they become so gracious? We have a theory. Most gracious people know Christ extremely well. They become like their gracious God, the Lord who is gracious and compassionate (see Exod. 34:6; 2 Chron. 30:9). One of the fascinating truths about life is that people become like the gods (or God) they worship and serve. Those who serve cruel "gods" such as bitterness, hate and revenge become cruel and violent. Those who serve lustful "gods" such as pornography or sexually explicit chat rooms become lustful and perverted. Those who serve materialistic "gods" such as money and greed become materialistic and selfish. Worse yet, these all become blind, deaf and dumb to the true God and His character qualities (see Pss. 115:4-8; 135:15-18).

The good news for Christians is that we serve a God of grace (see 1 Pet. 5:10). At the heart of His nature our Lord is gracious—merciful, peaceful, kind, patient and generous.

> AT THE HEART OF HIS NATURE OUR LORD IS GRACIOUS—MERCIFUL, PEACEFUL, KIND, PATIENT AND GENEROUS. HIS CHARACTER, OF COURSE, IS NOT LIMITED TO THESE QUALITIES, BUT GRACE IS ONE OF THE STUNNING DIAMONDS OF GOD'S NATURE.

His character, of course, is not limited to these qualities, but grace is one of the stunning diamonds of God's nature. What this means for committed Christians is that grace, together with its related character quality of graciousness, is ours because we live in union with Christ. The closer we draw to God, the more gracious we will become.

It is true that people with the spiritual gifts of mercy and hospitality may have a head start. But at its heart, graciousness is a character quality developed over a lifetime, not a gift given in a moment. Those who often speak gracious words of kindness, forgiveness or reconciliation attract powerful, influential friends (see Prov. 22:11). Those who speak foul, harsh or demanding words develop a mean spirit. Sadly, their selfishness robs them of friends and support when they need it most.

The gracious person finds that in the time of unresolved conflict God and friends give hope and help, just when it is needed most. "Even in darkness light dawns for the upright, for the gracious and compassionate and righteous man" (Ps. 112:4).

CHAPTER 12

WHEN YOU NEED TO KEEP THE PEACE

Thank God there are people in whose presence bitterness cannot live; people who bridge the gulfs, heal the breaches and sweeten the bitterness.

William Barclay, *The Gospel of Matthew*

Brad was a hospital administrator and also pastor of a small church (adapted from a true story, but names have been changed). His gifts for ministry were evident to all, and his enthusiasm was boundless. He worked hard, preached well, and the people loved him and his wife. He shared ministry with another couple, also bivocational, along with several committed leaders in the church. Together they made a first-rate team, and their small church was growing in numbers, enthusiasm and spiritual depth.

Peggy, a hospital employee, sought out Brad for counsel. She was having trouble in her personal life and in her marriage. Although she was highly effective at work, her sense of inner turmoil was driving her crazy. She had a history of adulterous affairs that were totally hidden from her husband, but now she wanted spiritual help. Over a period of months, Peggy and Brad met in his hospital office, and his wise insights were helpful to her. Back at church he was not hiding the fact that he loved what was happening. Then came the greatest joy of all, he led Peggy to receive Christ as Lord and Savior! Her husband began attending church along with her, the very church where Brad was pastor.

During the months of Brad's counseling with Peggy, one of the men at church confronted him kindly but firmly: "This relationship is getting too close. You need to back off."

"The blood of Christ will protect me," Brad replied. "Nothing bad is going to happen."

As more weeks went by, the concerned friend came back with one or two others to have a serious talk with Brad. They counseled him, "You are headed for trouble. You have to break off this relationship. How about asking one of the women in the church to spend time discipling her?" Brad agreed to having a godly woman take over discipling Peggy, but he kept meeting with her at the hospital. Since he was open about this, Brad thought it was okay. But the mood on the ministry team at church became tense and strained.

What Brad did not tell those who confronted him was that he was comforting Peggy in his office by holding her in his arms. Because they were not sleeping together, Brad kept saying, "The blood of Christ will protect me." Yet his conscience was bothering him. A time or two, Brad told Peggy that he needed to back away from their relationship. They were each married, after all, and should not be sharing this level of intimacy. In one of these tearful "break-up" sessions, Peggy began to unbutton her blouse, and Brad responded. They had committed full-on adultery before she left the office.

Brad loved the Lord, his wife and the church, and his conscience would not let him keep the adultery hidden. He confessed to his wife and to the ministry team at church. They called for a meeting with a denominational supervisor, and church discipline began. Brad was asked to resign from the church and become responsible to an accountability group. The terms of the church discipline required him to go for marriage counseling.

Brad resigned and began attending another congregation. Although it was painful and required continued urging from close Christian friends, he finally severed the relationship with Peggy. She also confessed to her husband, who immediately left the church, totally soured on Christians in general and pastors in particular. Brad and his wife began marriage counseling with a fine Christian therapist.

In time it came out that Brad had a long-standing battle with lust. While he had never engaged in physical adultery before Peggy, he had crossed the line of unacceptable behavior more than once. He joined a sexaholics group, and was surprised at how many other Christians were in it. Over a period of months, his defenses came down, and Christ's character began to be built up. Brad saved his marriage, in no small part due to a highly supportive wife. He stayed out of any kind of volunteer ministry for months. Only when the accountability group gave the green light did he move back into taking on service roles in his home church.

Brad became a winner. Even with the devastating consequences of his sin, he recovered personally and spiritually. He rebuilt his life, this time with far more humility and purity than before. But what if the church leaders had accepted his confession and swept the whole affair under the rug? It would have kept the peace—at least on the surface. Brad might still be the pastor there today, but given all the facts that came out later it is highly likely that the adultery would have repeated itself, maybe many times.

Jesus taught, "If he refuses to listen to them [the one or two others], tell it to the church; and if he refuses to listen even to the church, treat him as you would a pagan or a tax collector" (Matt. 18:17).

CHURCH DISCIPLINE

Why should any sin become public? Can't the Lord Himself deal with His own children? Doesn't public discipline make a scandal of the gospel? Shouldn't we just forgive and forget? Where's the role of grace? Can't the church practice what it preaches? Good questions.

Church discipline is a painful and touchy subject. Yet the church dare not ignore what the Bible teaches. No one is to judge another when the issue is a speck in a brother or sister's eye (see Matt. 7:1-5). However, the church is committed to judge when the matter is an open disgrace (see 1 Cor. 6:1-6; 1 Tim. 5:19-20). Church discipline for certain public sins is a command of Jesus and the New Testament (see Matt. 18:15-17; 1 Cor. 5:3-13). With a variety of actions to be taken, the Bible specifically names disorderly conduct, divisiveness, sexual immorality, false teaching, drunkenness, abusive speech, swindling and idolatry as issues requiring church discipline (see Rom. 16:17-18; 1 Cor. 6:9-11; 2 Thess. 3:6-15; 1 Tim. 1:20; 2 Tim. 2:17-18; Rev. 2:14-16).

> **WHY SHOULD ANY SIN BECOME PUBLIC? CAN'T THE LORD HIMSELF DEAL WITH HIS OWN CHILDREN?**

To pray passively, asking God to do what He has already commanded church leadership and parents to do, is to fail in God-given responsibilities. The purpose for discipline is threefold. First, it is to glorify God by protecting the honor of His reputation (see 1 Cor. 10:31-33). Scandalous sins that do not result in removal from official positions and the future protection of potential victims make Christ Jesus, the Head of the Church, look bad. Second, it is to carry out the ministry of reconciliation in restoring a Christian brother or sister caught in sin. (see Gal. 6:1). The goal is not to expose the sin, but to win back the offender. Third, the goal of discipline is to maintain the spiritual health of the church (see Acts 5:1-11; 1 Cor. 5:1-5; Heb. 12:10-12).

Far from making a scandal of the gospel, church discipline takes action to prevent future shame and disgrace. All Christians owe one another forgiveness, but trust must be earned. Church discipline gives time for restoring trust and rebuilding character. Since Jesus commanded the church to take action, His grace accompanies the process—at least for those who seek it. But if the church preaches grace while hiding the sins of its leaders, it falls into the scathing denunciations of hypocrisy from the lips of Jesus Himself.

Who Is Disciplined?
Most church discipline takes place in private. Pastors and church leaders confront situations with discretion and dignity. When it comes to public church discipline, discernment is what is needed regarding who should receive it. The key issue to ask is: Which way is this person going—toward Christ or away from Him? If the answer is that the person is moving toward Christ, then public church discipline is most often inappropriate. If the person is moving away from Christ, it is often evident in one's resistance to the discipline itself and to those in authority. Some situations are beyond debate. Immediate action must be taken in matters that are illegal and criminal or that endanger the health or safety of others.

When it comes to public church discipline, new Christians seldom if ever should receive it. They are growing in grace, trying to change their former way of life and working themselves out of problems from their non-Christian days.

When church discipline is needed for pastors, staff members or church leaders, appropriate action is essential. Most often they are asked to resign from office and are dropped from membership. If paid, they are released from service while honoring the terms of their contract. Contracts of employment can state that matters of church discipline void any agreements to further monetary payments. It is wise to state further that all parties agree as terms of the contract to engage in Christian mediation instead of going to court. (Such arrangements need to be in place *before* a problem requiring church discipline is discovered.)

Whose Responsibility?

Church policy—the agreed-upon procedures and practices in the constitution, bylaws, personnel handbook, official denominational publication or other official manual—will determine who has the final authority for disciplinary matters. Following these official rules is critical for legal protection as well as fairness to all the parties involved.

When it comes to confession of the sin, the basic principle for disciplinary procedures is that the circle of confession should be the same as the circle of sin. Private sins require private confession. Sins against whole groups require confession to that group. Only scandalous sins against the whole church require confession to the whole church.

The extent of the discipline depends on the attitude of the offender and the gravity of the offense. It may simply mean giving up certain positions of leadership until a matter is settled. More serious matters may call for suspension of membership. A few drastic cases require a total ban from the church buildings or grounds, such as in cases of child abuse, criminal sex offenses or threats of violence. The person is treated as "a pagan or a tax collector" (Matt. 18:17).

Appeal Process

To insure justice and fairness, it is wise for churches to set up an appeal process for those who vehemently disagree with an official church decision about discipline. Time limits for making the appeal can be clearly stated. The official group to review the decision should be stated, and whether or not that decision is final. Ground rules and official procedures are sometimes spelled out for the appeal.

Restoration

Since church discipline has reconciliation as its goal, it is wise to build into the official guidelines the possibility and general conditions for restoration. Typical requirements include the offender showing genuine signs of repentance, reconciliation and efforts at restitution if appropriate. Discipleship counseling provides personal guidance toward freedom in Christ. An accountability group set up to monitor progress is a must.

Legal Issues

The possibility of a church being taken to court because of church discipline toward members living in defiance of Scripture raises some important questions. The Bible says, "Be wise in the way you act toward outsiders" (Col 4:5; see also 1 Thess. 4:12; 1 Pet. 3:16-17). One major safeguard against legal action is "informed consent." Members of the church, especially all who first join, need to understand the congregation's written disciplinary policies. What is more, they need to sign a form that says church discipline was explained orally and in writing and that they consent to it should it ever become necessary.

People who win lawsuits against churches usually base their case on violation of one or more sensitive legal issues. The following guidelines should be reviewed by a Christian attorney for legal counsel regarding specific situations. Every church leader, however, will benefit by knowing in advance about these pitfalls.

- *Slander, libel or defamation of character is illegal.* Slanderous statements—true or untrue—are words intended to damage a person's reputation. The legal principle is that a matter must be communicated to a third party before it is considered slander. It is not slander or libel for official church leaders to confront a church member about a sin or a conflict. It is slander if they communicate it to others in a way that damages the person's reputation.
- *Invasion of privacy is illegal.* Church discipline by those charged with such responsibility is not invasion of privacy. Even so, caution is needed. Any public censure or excommunication proceedings must use fairly general terms. All statements, written and oral, need to be prepared carefully and fall in line with Scripture. Here is a sample letter used by one group:

> It has come to the attention of (the official group with authority) that one of the members of (church name) has violated the rules for voluntary membership and the standards of Scripture. All of the facts of the case are confirmed by two or more witnesses. Careful discussion with (name) has been undertaken to bring about reconciliation and restoration, but without success. Therefore, according to our stated procedures, (name) has been dropped from

membership (or the official body recommends that he or she be removed from membership) until these differences can be reconciled. This means that the disciplined member will not be allowed to participate in any way except (spell out any exceptions such as attendance at worship). We earnestly ask that this action not become a matter for personal offense or private gossip. If any members have questions, the (pastor and officially designated leaders) are willing to answer in private.

- *Inflicting a detrimental effect on a person's economic status is illegal.* The caution here is for churches not to go beyond their biblical limits of discipline. Dropping a person from church employment, membership and fellowship is legal. Inflicting economic harm by asking members not to do business with this person is not legal.
- *False imprisonment is illegal.* A person may not be held in a room, office, church or home without consent. Each person must always be free to leave at his or her own will and in the individual's own timing, without hindrance or coercion.

Wise Precautions

Disciplinary matters in the church are not to be settled in public courts (see 1 Cor. 6:1-11). Independent Christian mediation organizations may be helpful in resolving disputes (contact the Christian Legal Society in your area for referrals). The painful fact is that anyone can file a lawsuit against anyone else whenever desired. However unwarranted, the offended party may file a lawsuit against the church or its leaders. Filing and winning are two different matters, however. A church can do a few things to protect itself from losing a lawsuit.

- A local church can publish its standards of conduct and church discipline and communicate them to all members.
- A local church can communicate what steps of disciplinary action it may take and in what kinds of cases (see 1 Cor. 5).
- A local church can limit the number of people who are part of the process and give only general information to others (see Gal. 6:1; Eph. 5:15-16; Jas. 5:19-20).
- A local church can purchase workers compensation, liability and directors and officers insurance (sometimes called errors and omissions insurance).

Church discipline always seems painful, partly because no one can do it just right. No matter how wise and sensitive the action, some will criticize the leaders for acting too harshly, while others will feel offended that the church was so soft on sin. Other than revolutionary repentance and heart reconciliation based on the cross and resurrection of Jesus Christ, no human way of resolving sin's damage is fully available.

However, not all peacekeeping is as difficult as church discipline. Some kinds of peacemaking produce ever-widening circles of impact for Christ.

FROM CONFLICT TO FRIENDSHIP

Elie serves as pastor of the Friends Church in Kibimba, Burundi, where the Tutsi and Hutu tribes find ways to kill each other. Early missionaries built the large church, medical clinic, primary and secondary schools and dormitories that are used there. Although showing the signs of age, the facility is attractive and functional today. It also caught the eye of Tutsi soldiers during the recent war. They confiscated the complex for a military camp and occupied the buildings—including the sanctuary. This action only stoked the fire of vengeance already burning in the hearts of many Hutus. After six years, through the appeal of Swiss and American missionaries to the Burundian government, the buildings were finally given back to the church members.

Pastor Elie is a fine leader and a peacemaker. As a Hutu himself, the opposite tribe from the soldiers, he was smart enough not to take on the troops directly. Instead he looked for a childhood friend who was Tutsi. As a boy he had grown up in the Kibimba area and often played with Mattias, a Tutsi about his age. Their fathers knew each other and respected one another. Now, in spite of the tensions, Elie sought out Mattias as an ally in making peace rather than making war.

"Do you remember? We were friends before the war," said Elie.

"Yes, yes, I remember," replied Mattias.

"We need to do something and renew our friendship, so our friends and neighbors can survive."

The two men renewed their friendship just between the two of them. As they rebuilt trust, they encouraged others to cross tribal boundaries with the simple gift of being a friend. They did not try to build a big group, but intertribal friendships began to multiply. Over time, some 60 people were rebuilding trust with a member of the other tribe. That was when they were ready to organize. Their friendships had become the basis for action.

The term "peace committee" might not send shivers through the spines of people in the United States, but what these few people did was amazing! Members of both tribes began solving community problems, buying books for orphans and even building houses for widows—all in the midst of grinding poverty. They were peacemakers in a place where a spirit of vengeance reigned.[1]

PEACEMAKERS

The famous coach Knute Rockne once said, "One man practicing sportsmanship is far better than a hundred teaching it."[2] Elie and Mattias practiced more than sportsmanship; they practiced "peacemanship." In Chuck's devotional book, *More Energy for Your Day*, there is a fitting segment about today's peacemakers:

Peacemakers receive high marks from God.

Jesus said in the Sermon on the Mount, "Blessed are the peacemakers, for they will be called sons of God" (Matt. 5:9).

If Jesus were preaching in one of our pulpits today, I wonder if He might say something else.

"Blessed are the negotiators."

"Blessed are the mediators."

"Blessed are the reconcilers."

Peacemakers come in many forms—government negotiators, court-appointed mediators, marriage counselors, union-management arbitrators, church leaders. Some of the best peacemakers in the world are mothers.

It is not the title or the role that makes one a peacemaker, obviously, but rather the motivation and the skill.

Peacemakers quiet jangled nerves.

Peacemakers talk sense.

Peacemakers look for alternatives.

Peacemakers find common ground for agreement.

Peacemakers appeal for change.

Peacemakers negotiate.

Peacemakers work by the rules.

Peacemakers create new rules.

Peacemakers appeal to the powerful.

Peacemakers warn the vulnerable.

Peacemakers protect the weak.

Those who work for peace, using peaceful methods, often release new energy for good into relationships (see Jas. 3:18).

People in conflict feel better.

Marriages are put back together.

Working conditions improve.

Good legislation moves into operation.

Churches get outside of themselves.

Governments avoid war, and much, much more.

Peacemakers are not spineless, wishy-washy compromisers. Often they are people with strong convictions of their own. Even Jesus Christ, the greatest reconciler of all, once said, "Do not suppose that I have come to bring peace to the earth. I did not come to bring peace, but a sword" (Matt. 10:34).

The context shows that He was talking about acknowledging Him or disowning Him before others; following Him in spite of family pressure or failing Him; losing one's life for His sake or grasping onto one's own life and rejecting Him. Peacemakers do not pursue peace at any price. Instead they discern ways of making peace within the limits of

God's law,

cultural norms,

family understandings,

shared assumptions,

church rules,

company policy,

government regulations,

legal precedent.

Peacemakers do incredible good, especially when they are armed with the quiet power of the Prince of Peace.

George Fox once wrote,

"The peacemaker hath the kingdom and is in it;

and hath dominion over the peace-breaker

to calm him in the power of God."—from an epistle of 1652

"Turn from evil and do good; seek peace and pursue it" (Ps. 34:14).[3]

WADING IN ALLIGATORS

Peacemaking is not always easy, and neither is peacekeeping. No one wants to become ruthless, or turn into an appeaser. Winston Churchill once said, "An appeaser is one who feeds a crocodile, hoping it will eat him last."[4] Sometimes resolving a conflict feels like wading through a swamp. It is slow going, sticky and full of hungry alligators. We literally feel "swamped." When the alligators attack, when they get a grip on our flesh, when they start devouring us, we call for help (see Ps. 33:18-22). The Lord God Almighty is our refuge and strength, an ever-present help in trouble (see Ps. 46:1). The Holy Spirit is our Counselor and Helper (see John 14:15-16,26; 15:26; 16:7). Christ Jesus is the One who forgives us and teaches us to forgive others (see Matt. 6:14-15).

> **PEACEMAKING IS NOT ALWAYS EASY—AND NEITHER IS PEACEKEEPING.**

Somehow in His plan, God lets us wade with Him through the swamp of turmoil and confusion. We have commands to follow, wisdom to learn and love to give—even to our enemies (see Matt. 5:43-48). He is faithful, and He asks us to be true to Him and loving toward others (see Matt. 5:38-42). He promised to fight our battles for us (see Exod. 14:14; 1 Sam. 17:47). When you are wading in alligators, it takes everything you have to offer and all of Christ's grace you can muster.

- Keep your priorities straight: Build a bridge over the swamp.
- Laugh and love and live as you go: Smile through your tears.
- Bring in other people whenever possible, wherever appropriate: Never take on alligators alone.
- Monitor progress daily: Keep your eye on Christ's activity, and join Him.
- Walk in wisdom: Look to God and His Word.

PEACEKEEPERS

Some people are conflict prone, some families dysfunctional, some businesses litigious, some churches full of conflict. What is fascinating is that others nearby are not. In the same kinds of circumstances other people are reconciliation prone, other families fully functional, other businesses harmonious and other churches peaceful. What makes the difference? Often it is the leadership—men and women who serve well as peacekeepers—not as thought police or ruthless dictators but as morale builders and problem solvers. Let us review a few steps often adopted by effective peacekeepers:

- *Create a climate full of love and joy.* Love one another—and your enemies. Go the second mile. Say only what is helpful. Speak the soft word that turns away anger.

Show respect. Yield on an issue. Honor one another above yourselves.

- *Calm a quarrel instead of starting one.* Use wisdom to extinguish a little blaze of conflict when it first ignites. Never repeat gossip. Refuse to take up an offense for someone else. Stay out of quarrels that are not your own.

- *Use the right bucket.* When the glitch hits, when complaints surface, wise Christians carry two buckets—water and gasoline. They learn to pour water on angry blazes and gasoline on the fire of the Holy Spirit, not vice versa.

- *Get past the conflict and on with your life.* Forgive as the Lord forgave you. Let it go. Give thanks in all circumstances. Bless those who mistreat you. Never try to get even. Let the person off your hook, knowing no one will get off of God's hook.

- *Make every dispute a learning opportunity.* Grow in wisdom. Refuse to repeat mistakes—yours or others that you observe. Good judgment comes by learning from bad experiences. In the middle of a conflict, just get through it with Christ's help, always seeking full reconciliation. Later, reflect on it and pray for the Lord to reveal what He taught you.

What is called for here is *prudence*. Most people who use the term "prudent" today associate it with a financial investment. People want to be careful about their money. They do not want to squander it, mismanage it or even have a potentially good investment go bad. But when we read in the Bible about being prudent, it has to do with character, behavior, wisdom in everyday life. It shows up most often in Proverbs. "A simple man believes anything, but a prudent man gives thought to his steps"

(Prov. 14:15). "A prudent man sees danger and takes refuge, but the simple keep going and suffer for it" (Prov. 22:3).

Prudent people are careful, cautious, practical. They bypass glitzy instant gratification and look for long-term benefits. They avoid foolish mistakes whenever possible. The result? They become respected and wise. One typical fruit of prudence is prosperity. What is more, they do it honestly and to the benefit of those around them. Better than material wealth is a biblical way of life that emerges.

- Their friends know they are trustworthy.
- They take the right steps—in advance.
- They make good choices.
- Their counsel is invaluable.
- They give real help to people in need.

When prudence is combined with a lifestyle of blessing others in Christ's name, the result is undeniably powerful.

BLESSING

Some people go through life cursing—people, events, circumstances. Others go through life blessing—loving, encouraging, doing good. Sometimes we have Christian forms of cursing—complaining, gossiping, withdrawing. We can also discover Christian ways of blessing—praying, praising, reconciling. It makes a world of difference whether we go through life cursing those around us, or blessing them. Those who curse leave a trail of misery, unhappiness and damaged relationships. Those who bless leave a legacy of help, love and joy.

The pressure and pain of conflict may bring either cursing or blessing to the top. When some people get mad, or get hurt, they respond with curses. But under the same circumstances, others respond with blessings. When things do not go our way, when people hurt us, when life seems unfair, do we bless or curse? As we walk by others at work or school, or drive by our neighbors' houses, do we pray down blessings or grumble about their lifestyle?

The Bible makes it quite clear that followers of Jesus are to go through life blessing, especially blessing their enemies.

- Bless those who curse you (Luke 6:28).
- Bless those who persecute you; bless and do not curse (Rom. 12:14).
- When we are cursed, we bless (1 Cor. 4:12).

Who is most apt to hear our witness of Christ? Someone whom we have blessed and shown kindness to or someone we have cursed by our criticism and complaints? Who is most hindered from coming to Christ? Someone among our families or friends that we have reconciled with, or someone who still feels we hurt them or did them wrong?

Please do not misunderstand. We should hate the deceitful world system that drags people into sin with its damage and death. At the same time we can bless the individuals involved. We can pray down God's blessings upon them—health and healing, employment and achievement, joy and peace, family and friends, salvation and worship. We all believe that God answers prayer. It follows that if we pray down a blessing upon others, it will make a tangible difference.

Through it all we must always remind ourselves that our present troubles are only for a moment. Eternal rewards await those who trust Christ and are faithful (see 2 Cor. 4:16-18). Bridges of the Kingdom are being built, and one day the faithful will walk over them into the Kingdom of glory! (see Col. 1:13-14).

Alligators, beware!

Daily Prayers for Times of Conflict

Monday

Lord, You commanded us to consider it pure joy when we face trials of many kinds. That's because perseverance leads us to become mature and complete in Christ, and that's something to rejoice about. The Bible clearly commands, "Be joyful always; pray continually; give thanks in all circumstances, for this is God's will for you in Christ Jesus" (1 Thess. 5:16-17). Help me, Lord. Cause me to create this joyful, prayerful, thankful climate in every part of my life and influence—my home, workplace, friendships and in relationships with those who oppose me.

I claim Your hedge of protection, including the full armor of God and the angels of God. I put on the belt of truth, the breastplate of righteousness, the boots of readiness that come from the gospel of peace, the shield of faith, the helmet of salvation and the sword of the Spirit which is the (spoken) word of God. Keep me praying in the Spirit on all occasions, and with all kinds of requests. Help me always to keep on praying for all the saints. I pray for Your blessings on those who are giving me such a hard time. Work in their lives, too, in ways that will accomplish Your good pleasure and eternal purposes.

I especially thank and praise You for revealing Yourself and saving me through the life, death and resurrection of our Lord Jesus Christ. Thank You for Your sacrificial love, sending Him to die for all of us (including the contentious people in my life) and for all of our sins. He rose again for our justification, to give us newness of life. I praise You that our risen Lord Jesus Christ reigns at Your right hand in the place of supreme honor, glory and authority. I glorify You, exalt You, worship You.

Since we will all stand before the judgment seat of Christ, get me ready for this second most important day of my life. Give me a heart like Jesus now, so that on that Day I will hear His "Well done, good and faithful servant" (Matt. 25:21). Thank You that the best is yet to come. And thank You that Your compassions are new every morning. Pour them into my heart today and every day. You know how much I need You right now.

TUESDAY

Thank You that You are the Father of compassion and the God of all comfort. Thank You that You suffered and died for my sorrows and weaknesses as well as for my sins (see Isa. 53:4-5). I praise You that You heal all my diseases and redeem my life from the pit (see Ps. 103:1-3). Do the same for those on the other side of this conflict. Thank You that You remove Satan's footholds and strongholds as I submit to You, resist the devil and draw near to You again. Thank You for the freedom in Christ that You give me. I pray for those who spitefully use me, that You will bring them to full freedom in Christ as well.

By grace through faith I bring around me and within me all the redemptive effects of the cross of Christ, the blood of Christ and the atoning sacrifice of the Lord Jesus Christ. With excitement I claim His ransom from sin, release from guilt, relief from the sinful nature, renewal of righteousness and removal of shame.

I accept the light of Christ and will walk in the light as He is in the light. Thank You for Your power over the evil one, Your authority to break ongoing cycles of destructive behavior and Your victory over all the evil forces in the heavenly realms. Thank You for abundant, eternal life—both present and future.

I rejoice that You are the God of grace, mercy, peace, kindness, patience, forbearance, humility, gentleness, acceptance, forgiveness, submission, consideration, courtesy, sympathy, dignity, generosity and rest. Because I am Your child, I gladly welcome these gifts of character in my life. As it would please You, bless my opponents with these character qualities as well. Thank You that by Your grace I am saved, reconciled, accepted and forgiven. Through Your grace I put to death any and every way my old life might violate grace, such as selfishness, hoarding, impatience, irritability, anger, resentment, unforgiveness, bitterness, contempt, condemnation, legalism, racism and cruelty.

Make me a grace-filled person, full of the grace of Jesus. May Your gracious attitudes and nonverbal communication fill my actions, attitudes, words and especially my thoughts about my adversaries! Fill me afresh with the Spirit of grace so I will be accepting, understanding, agreeable, compassionate, kind, humorous, winsome, supportive, merciful and freeing. Make me fun to live with, work with, be with. If it would please You, run some of Your surprises of grace through me to delight others! May Your grace in this vessel, this temple, overflow to all around me so they give praise and glory to our Lord Jesus Christ.

WEDNESDAY

Protect me from distortions of truth that my opponents are spreading—rumors, innuendos, gossip, lies, slander. Through my life and the lives of all Your people, win the spiritual warfare against the devil, the flesh and the world. Help me to discern deception in my own perception from any source and to bring it into the light. Dismiss Satan's lies from my mind. Protect me from the evil one.

I pray especially for those who oppose me now but will one day turn to You with authentic repentance and saving faith in our Lord Jesus Christ (see John 17:20). May we all become one in Christ. Display Your glory through me and through them. Glorify Yourself in ways that are unique to me and to them—ways You purposed for us from before the foundation of the world.

I rejoice that You are the God of truth, wisdom, knowledge, understanding, discernment, insight, instruction, ideas, sound judgment, faithfulness, steadfastness, reliability, impartiality, honesty, wholesome thinking, prudence and discretion. Because I am Your child, I welcome these character qualities into my life. Thank You that by Your truth I am free and that I am established, rooted and grounded in my identity in Christ. Through Your truth, I put to death any and all rationalizations, dishonesty, lies, deceit, confusion, foolish thinking, bondage, worldly wisdom, spiritual blindness and every other lie from the evil one.

Deliver me from complaining, grumbling, negative attitudes, irritability, accusatory tones, judgmental statements, critical words, know-it-all answers and attitudes, "I'm right" posturing, superiority feelings and judgmental thoughts. Open my eyes to see that these come from my flesh, my sinful nature, and not from the Holy Spirit. Set me free from them. Teach me the wisdom not to accuse my opponents or even suggest they are wrong, but, instead, to find tactful ways to explore the truth together.

THURSDAY

Protect me from distortions of love such as becoming an enabler of people's addictions, a sick codependent who tries to protect them from the consequences of their sinful actions. Teach me to discern between authentic self-giving love that redeems sinners and phony selfish love that enables more sin. Keep me alert to avoid "give to get" substitutes for love.

I rejoice that You are the God of love, compassion, friendship, affection, caring, companionship, closeness, intimacy, warmth, tenderness, gratitude, rejoicing, laughter, tears, delight, service, sacrifice, self-giving, cherishing, encouragement and edification. Because I am Your child, I welcome these character qualities into my life. Thank You that because of Your love I am fully loved and made complete in Your joy. Through Your love I put to death every hint of apathy, hardness of heart, holding others at arm's length, jealousy, hatred, fear, selfishness, self-pre-occupation, self-indulgence, self-pity, harsh and hurtful words. Work on my opponents' hearts to do the same.

I thank You for Your passionate, covenant love that flows from You to me and from You to those I disagree with. I pray that Your kind of passionate love will flow back again from me to You, and will overflow to others, even to "them." Fill me with Your love, Your self-giving love. Cause me to love my enemies as I love myself, to love them by faith with Your love. Give me Your compassion for deceived and disillusioned people who are so antagonistic.

FRIDAY

Protect me from distortions of power that the other side is misusing to get their own way. Teach me the peacemaking strategies that will restore harmony. When I feel afraid to act, or hesitate because I might overreact, help me to appropriate Your divine power and authority. Teach me to use it wisely just as Jesus would.

I rejoice that You are the God of strength, energy, might, forcefulness, working, action, zeal, self-control, responsibility, discipline, perseverance, endurance, long-suffering, contentment, confidence, courage, boldness, motivation, morale and momentum. Because I am Your child, I welcome these character qualities into my life. Thank You that through Your power I am energized, significant and capable. Through Your power I put to death any attitudes or actions such as timidity, moral weakness, laziness, cowardice, passivity, giving up, giving in, not finishing well, no self-control, bad habits, addictions, discontent, complaining, grumbling, murmuring, conflict, strife, ruthlessness, rage and abuse.

Give me Your power in prayer, and raise up godly intercessors who will pray for me during this difficult time.

SATURDAY

Thank You, Lord, that You are a God of justice. You will judge my enemies—and me. Prepare me for our Lord Jesus Christ's second coming in power and great glory. As I wait for His appearing, lead me to purify myself as He is pure. Teach me to rejoice as I worship, wait, work, rest, give, serve, do good and treat my adversaries with love so that daily I live in the light of Jesus Christ's return. Fill me with holy anticipation of that great event, of the final judgment that will destroy the earth with fire and give entrance to the eternal rewards of the new heaven and new Earth, the home of righteousness—or the terrible alternative of eternal condemnation. I look forward to our Lord Jesus Christ's appearing and to our resurrection bodies that will be like His glorious body. Give me a balanced, two-age perspective on this present evil age so that I am looking forward to the age to come.

I rejoice that You are the God of holiness, righteousness, justice, fairness, purity, integrity, blamelessness, spotlessness, goodness, godliness, virtue, sincerity, single-mindedness, consecration, uprightness, reverence and respect. Because I am Your child, I welcome these character qualities into my life. Thank You that through Your holiness and by Your Holy Spirit I am cleansed, consecrated and satisfied. In right relationship with You, I am set apart for You and Your sacred purposes. I am made holy, sharing the character and imitating the conduct of Jesus Christ. Your Word says, "God made him who had no sin to be sin for us, so that in him we might become the righteousness of God" (2 Cor. 5:21). Through Your holiness, I put to death the old life of selfishness, double-mindedness, hypocrisy, neglecting worship, irreverence, injustice, foul language, ridicule, foolishness, scoffing, mocking, lewdness and every other sin. Remove my silly excuses not to obey You. Help me to live a holy life and to keep idols from setting up a throne in my heart.

Keep me alert to secular substitutes for holiness, such as trying to be good enough on my own ("I'm a pretty good person") or projecting a good image ("It's how you look that matters," "You have to keep up appearances"). Prevent me from falling into denial that anything is my fault, and protect me from any and every defense mechanism ("I can't help it," "It's just the way I am," "That's just me," "It's my disease kicking in") that excuses sinful behavior. Keep convicting the consciences of my adversaries about these issues as well.

SUNDAY

You give so much more from the storehouse of Your eternal wealth. I welcome Your forgiveness, cleansing, gifts, fruit, character, satisfaction, fellowship, light, life and freedom. Thank You that I am a child of God, a new creation in Christ—delighted, rejoicing and growing. I welcome Your Name, blessings, promises, covenant, kingdom, lordship, fullness, likeness, inheritance, unity, oneness and wholeness. Thank You for answers to prayer. Thank You that I am in Christ and that Christ is in me. I put to death dependence on myself and my own resources, my stubborn refusal to live constantly connected to Christ. Instead, I depend upon, abide in and remain with Jesus Christ our Lord. I live in Christ, with Christ, for Christ, by Christ and through Christ.

Cause me to respond to You, to Your resources and Your riches with revolutionary repentance, with resurrection faith, resurrection hope, resurrection love and resurrection holy obedience. Teach me to renew my mind, set my thoughts on things above, fix my thoughts on Jesus, so that my thinking about You, my following You, my working with You and my witnessing about You are in Christ and Spirit filled. Through me, magnify Your Name.

Use me to reconcile the deep divisions that I face. I acknowledge that You are the ultimate reconciler between individuals, ethnic groups, Jews and Gentiles, male and female, enslaved and free. Bring everything in heaven and on earth under one head, our Lord Jesus Christ. Make all the people of God one in Christ Jesus. Cause the love that the Father has for Jesus to be in them and in us, and Your very self in us.

DECLARATION

In Christ and His authority I stand against the evil one (see Eph. 6:10-20) and his lies, attacks, influence, harassment, hindrances, distractions, confusion, divisiveness, criticism, gossip, doubts, discouragement, disillusionment, depression, loneliness, despair, temptations, accusations, condemnation, contempt, judgmentalism, deceptions, blindness, degrading mental images, rage, curses, generational consequences, nightmares, sleeplessness, physical attacks, assaults, kidnappings, persecution and every other means of Satan and his evil powers and authorities against me and those I love. I submit to God and resist the devil in any and every place that I am vulnerable.

O heavenly Father, Lord Jesus Christ, Holy Spirit—the triune God—remove every place, every foothold and stronghold, every crack and crevice that the evil one uses to take hold of me. Fill me with Your Holy Spirit, clothe me in Christ. Keep me obedient to Your command: "Be joyful always; pray continually; give thanks in all circumstances, for this is God's will for you in Christ Jesus" (1 Thess. 5:16-18).

In the powerful name of the Lord Jesus Christ.

Amen.

Seven Steps Toward Biblical Reconciliation

Step 1: Image of God Versus Sinful Nature

Each person lists the good things—strengths, qualities and character of the other person. Each one states them aloud to the other.

The Bible says we were all created in the image of God (see Gen. 1:27). Although sin tarnished that image, we all retain some character strengths and positive qualities. This step acknowledges who we are in Christ, image-bearers of our creator and redeemed children of God. Everyone has strengths and weaknesses—*everyone*! This is the time to state the strengths.

Begin with everyone present praying aloud together:

Heavenly Father,
Thank You that every person was created in Your image. Bring to
our minds the strengths, abilities and character qualities of each
other. Give us grace to speak these truths honestly and sincerely.
In Jesus' name, amen.

STEP 2: GOOD MEMORIES VERSUS BLANKED-OUT MEMORIES

Each person rehearses aloud the good memories from their relationship in the past.

Conflict, especially among Christians, most often comes out of a prior relationship. Some antagonists used to feel like brothers and sisters in Christ. They may have worked together in the cause of Christ, enjoyed great social times, grown up together or been part of the same family. Those relationships and experiences have built some positive memories. Before addressing any of the current problems, each one recalls good memories from their past. This exercise builds up their emotional bank accounts and helps prepare for the more painful withdrawals to follow.

Note: It is important to not only state the items each one mentions in Steps 1 and 2, but to also *write them down.*

Begin this step by everyone praying together:

Heavenly Father,
Thank You for the good memories from our past experiences.
Bring them to our minds right now, so we can share them in a
constructive way. Cause us to rejoice in these good memories and
to obey Your command to "give thanks in all circumstances, for
this is God's will for you in Christ Jesus" (1 Thess. 5:18).
In Jesus' name, amen.

STEP 3: VERBALIZED PAIN VERSUS HIDDEN PAIN

Each person names the failures and painful memories that have damaged their relationship, beginning with their earliest memories. By the end of this step, each one will respond by telling the other, "From your description of what happened, I can now see how I hurt you. I was wrong [or sinned against you] in (specifically name the offense)." Both parties must acknowledge what they have done that hurt the other person and acknowledge their own part in the offense. At the end of this step, *both people pray and confess before God their own part in the conflict.*

Ever since Adam and Eve fell into sin, all the rest of humanity have followed in their footsteps (see Gen. 3; Rom. 3:23). No one is perfect. All have sinned. Everyone has flaws, character defects and weaknesses. In any conflict, something happened to trigger the trouble. It could be a series of events or a persistent sin or weakness, such as adultery, rage, gossip, criticism or misunderstanding. Sometimes the conflict involves a material issue, such as a broken contract, real estate matter, unpaid loan, child custody argument, personal injury or landlord-renter dispute. Acknowledging our sins, wrongdoings or faults against another person is often a big step toward reconciliation; however, first those sins must be heard from the viewpoint of the one who feels wronged.

Begin this step by praying together:

> *Heavenly Father,*
> *Give us insight into each other's pain. Grant us eyes to see,*
> *ears to hear and a heart of compassion. Help us to com-*
> *municate with accuracy and honesty so that the facts*
> *and feelings will become clear to all.*
> *In Jesus' name, amen.*

The following is an example of how this step might unfold:

One of the two in conflict begins by sharing their earliest painful memory. The second person listens without interruption. When the first one is finished describing his or her viewpoint of the sin, abuse, disappointment or emotional pain, the second person can ask for clarification if necessary. Sometimes the facilitator may want to ask the listener to repeat what was said, including the intensity of feeling, so the first person feels heard. Then the second person responds with his or her own account of the same incident.

The first person proceeds to the next memory. It often helps to follow a time line with the oldest painful memories first. After each incident recalled, the second person rehearses the same memory from a personal point of view.

When the first person finishes recounting all the recalled painful memories, reverse roles. The second person goes through any painful memories not yet mentioned. The first person then responds with his or her own memory of the incident. This gives new perspective to both people in the conflict. They hear the other person's story and the hurt that it caused. By beginning with the earliest memories, the pain is diminished somewhat because usually the memories are more distant.

After listening, each person acknowledges his or her own wrong to the other. First one and then the other says, "From your description of what happened, I can now see how I hurt you. I was wrong [or sinned against you] in (specifically name the offense)." Both parties must acknowledge what they have done that hurt the other person and acknowledge their own part in the offense.

At the end of this step both people pray and confess before God their own part in the conflict.

For Christians, confessing to God is an effective way to clear the air of misunderstanding and unhappiness.

STEP 4: SEEKING FORGIVENESS VERSUS CLAIMING INNOCENCE

Each person asks forgiveness of the other, saying aloud, "I was wrong. Will you forgive me for what I did when I (name the hurts, disappointments, wrongs and sins)?" Encourage both parties to ask forgiveness from the other. Lasting reconciliation will seldom come without asking for and receiving forgiveness. It gives each a fresh start, an opportunity to change for the better.

Begin this step by praying together:

Heavenly Father,
Help us get in touch with the pain of this conflict, so that we may
ask forgiveness of one another from the heart. Keep us from
mouthing religious words that we don't mean. Make our seek-
ing and giving of forgiveness as real as Jesus' forgiveness of us.
In Jesus' name, amen.

STEP 5: STATED COMMITMENTS VERSUS WISHFUL THINKING

Each person tells the other, "Before the Lord, I am going to do my best to become the person God created me to be. In the spirit of Christian love, I will do or will stop doing the following in regard to our relationship (state specific actions)." If helpful, the other may respond with

"It would make it easier for me to follow through on our reconciliation if you would/would not (state a specific desired action)."

Stating specific commitments in a spirit of love can help to clarify expectations. It replaces wishful thinking and hoping for the best. Speaking the truth in love nudges each one from forgiveness toward lasting change. Each person in a conflict needs to hear what the other is willing to do or to stop doing.

When material issues are involved, this is the time for brainstorming. Encourage both to come up with possible solutions to their problem. Write these thoughts down, looking for one idea to stimulate another. Explain that evaluating the ideas comes later. At this point, it is off-limits to criticize anything mentioned, no matter how far-fetched or unreasonable it may sound. Gather as many suggestions as possible. When the brainstorming is complete, work together to select the best ideas.

Begin this step by praying together:

Heavenly Father,
Give us each wisdom and insight into what to do in order to live
as the person You intend for us to become. Give us determina-
tion to do our best before You. Also show us how to ask
for what we really need from each other.
In Jesus' name, amen.

STEP 6: COVENANT OF AGREEMENT VERSUS HARDENED POSITIONS

The two talk together about what they are willing to agree to. If a material issue is involved, the two discuss possible ways to settle the dispute (you can use the brainstorming list from the previous step). As they reach agreement on each issue, with the guiding wisdom of the one or two others, they put it into a covenant of agreement before God. Both sign this covenant.

A covenant between adversaries is a biblical and time-honored way of building a lasting peace (see Gen. 31:44). Simply hearing the other person's commitments and desires for change is good. Reaching an agreement and putting it in writing as a covenant is even better. Evaluate the commitments, desires, ideas and solutions mentioned in the last step, looking for the best solutions for both parties. Pray in faith for God's wisdom.

If the previous steps were not successful, then the goal of reconciliation is not possible. However, the lesser goal of reaching a workable compromise or mediating a truce may still be possible. When conflict cannot be transformed into reconciliation, it may yet be negotiated into a workable agreement.

If agreement does not come easily, it may well be time for some personal coaching, asking each participant to step outside for a moment. Sometimes one of those in the conflict will share facts or feelings with the facilitator that they will not say face-to-face in the group. The facilitator and prayer partner may need to encourage adoption of one of the better solutions, urge a reasonable compromise or suggest a negotiation strategy. If one person is far more dominant than the other or in a powerful position of authority, the facilitator must be careful to keep the process fair to both.

Add as many agreements as are needed. Something about writing down the original strengths shared at the beginning of the session and writing the agreement at this point makes the reconciliation easier to review. *Each person should sign the covenant when it is concluded.*

Begin this step by praying together:

Heavenly Father,
Grant us full biblical reconciliation, the kind that makes us one
in Christ and brings us to agreement. As we put our covenant
into writing, may Your stamp of approval rest upon it. Remind
us that we will answer to You for keeping this covenant when
we stand before the judgment seat of Christ (see 2 Cor. 5:10).
In Jesus' name, amen.

STEP 7: BLESSINGS VERSUS RESENTMENTS

Each person prays blessings, thanksgiving and praise upon
the other.

Jesus taught us to love our enemies, to do good to those who
hate us, to pray for those who mistreat us and to bless those who
curse us (see Luke 6:27-28). What better time to obey Him than
at the close of a reconciliation session? This puts Christ's positive touch upon each other and upon the relationship from this
point on. Each person should pray blessings on the other.

Heavenly Father,
We bless each other with every spiritual blessing in Christ Jesus.
We thank You for reconciliation to Yourself and to one another.
Protect our future relationship with one another and our
agreement for action. May what happened here today
bring praise, honor and glory to God.
In Jesus' name, amen.

CONCLUSION

The list of strengths and good memories from Steps 1 and 2,
along with the written Covenant from Step 7, should be copied

for each participant, including the facilitator and prayer partner.

The facilitator explains that one reconciliation session does not prevent future conflict (as we all know from marriage and family relationships). It is important now for each to give the other person permission to speak the truth with great love and tenderness when future conflicts arise.

Leave thanking God that He has provided reconciliation through Jesus Christ our Lord.

TIPS FOR THE FACILITATOR AND PRAYER PARTNER

1. Greet the people warmly and thank them for coming to work toward a fair, honest, just solution. Remind them that we will be in Christ's presence as we go through the Steps to Reconciliation.

2. Set the ground rules. Each one will have a turn to explain his or her viewpoint, so listen carefully when the other person is talking. No interruptions, please. The facilitator will guide the process and "play referee" when and if it is necessary. All language and communication are to be polite and respectful. Explain that by the conclusion of the session, we hope to reach a *mutually acceptable* agreement.

3. From time to time, the facilitator or prayer partner may take each party aside for a brief personal discussion. Either party may also request this time out at any point in the process (e.g., when emotions become too heated or when it appears things are bogged down). Sometimes one party will need some personal

counsel about flexibility, giving ground, misunder-standing, sticking to the agreed ground rules or some other obvious issue. A good question for the facilitator to begin a personal conference is "At this point in the process, how do you feel it is going?"

4. Ask each person involved to use "I" statements when explaining his or her feelings—even when explaining the painful memories.

5. Do not allow interruptions or accusations. When they occur, stop them, even in midsentence.

6. Keep on track and don't wander away from the process, unless the Holy Spirit is doing some remark-able work in His own way.

7. Make sure each person has the opportunity to speak openly and honestly but without using manipulative, deceptive or unacceptable behaviors. This calls for each person to use simple common sense and to agree in advance to live by the ground rules and let the facilitator "play referee" when needed.

ENDNOTES

Introduction

1. Joe Wasmond is now the president of Freedom in Christ Ministries.
2. Neil T. Anderson, *Released from Bondage*, 2nd ed. (Nashville, TN: Thomas Nelson, 2002).
3. Lewis B. Smedes, *Forgive and Forget* (San Francisco: Harper and Row, 1984), pp. 119-120.

Chapter 1

1. Neil T. Anderson and Robert Saucy, *God's Power at Work in You* (Eugene, OR: Harvest House, 2001), p. 42. We encourage you to consider this book for a comprehensive understanding of sanctification.

Chapter 2

1. Neil T. Anderson, *Who I Am in Christ* (Ventura, CA: Regal Books, 2001), p. 278.
2. For information specifically directed at resolving personal and spiritual conflicts on an individual basis, see Anderson and Mylander, *Helping Others Find Freedom in Christ* (Ventura, CA: Regal Books, 1995). For information directed at resolving marital conflicts, see Anderson and Mylander, *The Christ-Centered Marriage* (Ventura, CA: Regal Books, 1996). For information directed at corporate conflict resolution in ministries, see Anderson and Mylander, *Setting Your Church Free* (Ventura, CA: Regal Books, 1994).

Chapter 3

1. Martin Luther King, Jr., *A Testament of Hope: The Essential Writings of Martin Luther King, Jr.* (Washington, DC: Sojourners, 1992), p. 81.
2. Cain Hope Felder, *Race, Racism and the Biblical Narratives* (Minneapolis, MN: Fortress Press, 1991), pp. 129-132, 146-153.
3. E. Stanley Jones, *Mahatma Gandhi: An Interpretation* (New York: Abingdon-Cokesbury Press, 1948), p. 54.
4. Gordon W. Allport, *The Nature of Prejudice* (Reading, PA: Addison-Wesley, 1979), p. 456.
5. Dorothy Sayer, quoted in Philip Yancey, *The Jesus I Never Knew* (Grand Rapids, MI: Zondervan Publishing House, 1995), p. 23.
6. Curtiss Paul DeYoung, *Reconciliation, Our Greatest Challenge—Our Only Hope* (Valley Forge, PA: Judson Press, 1997), pp. 37-38.
7. Irenaeus, *Against Heresies*, v. 24.3.
8. Ernest Wright, *The Challenge of Israel's Faith* (London: SCM Press, 1946), p. 92.

9. Johannes Pedersen, *Israel: Its Life and Culture*, vol. 1-2 (London: Oxford University Press, 1926), p. 308.

10. L. Kohler, *Theologie des Alten Testaments* (Tubingen, Germany: n.p., 1947), p. 113.

11. Eric Fromm, *The Art of Loving* (New York: Harper and Row, 1956), pp. 6-7.

Chapter 4

1. Clyde Kirby, *Then Came Jesus* (Grand Rapids, MI: Zondervan, 1967).

2. To understand the theological basis for these Steps and to understand how to properly use them, read Anderson, *Helping Others Find Freedom in Christ* (Ventura, CA: Regal Books, 1995).

3. Neil T. Anderson and Rich Miller, *Getting Anger Under Control* (Eugene, OR: Harvest House, 2002).

4. Neil T. Anderson, *A Way of Escape* (Eugene, OR: Harvest House, 1994).

Chapter 5

1. Dietrich Bonhoeffer, *The Cost of Discipleship*, trans. R. H. Fuller (New York: Macmillan, 1963), p. 100.

Chapter 7

1. David Niyonzima and Lon Fendall, *Unlocking Horns: Forgiveness and Reconciliation in Burundi*, (Newberg, OR: Barclay Press, 2001).

2. Ibid., pp. 1-11.

3. Ken Sande, *The Peacemaker*, rev. ed. (Grand Rapids, MI: Baker Books, 1997), p. 24.

4. Carolyn Schrock-Shenk and Lawrence Ressler, eds., *Making Peace with Conflict: Practical Skills for Conflict Transformation* (Scottsdale, PA: Herald Press, 1999), p. 23.

5. Henry Wadsworth Longfellow, quoted in Eugene Ehrlich and Marshall DeBruhl, *The International Thesaurus of Quotations, Revised and Updated*, vol. 1 (New York: Harper Perennial, 1996), p. 190 (288.16).

Chapter 8

1. For a lengthier and more academic explanation of similar processes, see David W. Augsburger, *Conflict Mediation Across Cultures, Pathways and Patterns* (Louisville, KY: Westminster/John Knox Press, 1992), pp. 234-248.

2. Neil T. Anderson and Charles Mylander, *Setting Your Church Free* (Ventura, CA: Regal Books, 1994).

3. Philip Keller, *A Shepherd Looks at Psalm 23* (Minneapolis, MN: World Wide Publications, 1970), pp. 122-124.

4. Augsburger, p. 243.

Chapter 9

1. For detailed information about these steps, see Neil Anderson, *The Steps to Freedom* (Ventura, CA: Regal Books, 2001). For the marriage-focused Steps

to Freedom, see Anderson and Mylander, *The Christ-Centered Marriage: Discovering and Enjoying Your Freedom in Christ Together* (Ventura, CA: Regal Books, 1996), pp. 249-281. For the church-focused Steps to Freedom, see Anderson and Mylander, *Setting Your Church Free: A Biblical Plan to Help Your Church* (Ventura, CA: Regal Books, 1994), Appendix B.

2. Anderson and Mylander, *Setting Your Church Free,* pp. 324-325.

3. Marshall Shelley, *Well-Intentioned Dragons: Ministering to Problem People in the Church,* (Carol Stream, IL: Christianity Today; Waco, TX: Word Books, 1985), p. 110.

Chapter 10

1. For an explanation of these ways, see Ken Sande, *The Peacemaker, A Biblical Guide to Resolving Personal Conflict,* rev. ed. (Grand Rapids, MI: Baker Books, 1997), pp. 16-21.

2. Ken Sande and Ted Kober, *Guiding People Through Conflict* (Billings, MT: Peacemaker Ministries, 1998), p. 4.

Chapter 11

1. Marshall Shelley, *Well-Intentioned Dragons: Ministering to Problem People in the Church* (Carol Stream, IL: Christianity Today; Waco, TX: Word Books, 1985), p. 125.

2. Neil T. Anderson, *The Steps to Freedom in Christ,* rev. ed. (Ventura, CA: Gospel Light, 2001).

3. We recommend Peacemaker Ministries, which also has a network of affiliated mediators in various parts of the country. You can contact Peacemaker Ministries by post at 1537 Avenue D, Suite 352, Billings, MT 59102; by phone at (406) 256-1583; by fax at (406) 256-0001; through their website at www.HisPeace.org or by e-mail at mail@HisPeace.org.

4. A comprehensive secular resource for conflict resolution is Christopher W. Moore, *The Mediation Process: Practical Strategies for Resolving Conflict,* 2nd ed. (San Francisco: Jossey-Bass, 1996).

5. Ken Sande and Ted Kober, *Guiding People Through Conflict* (Billings, MT: Peacemaker Ministries, 1998), p. 21.

Chapter 12

1. Personal interview with Pastor Elie in Bujumbura, Burundi, 31 August, 2001.

2. Knute Rockne, quoted in *Great Quotes from Great Leaders,* comp. Peggy Anderson (Lombard, IL: Celebrating Excellence Publishing, 1990), p. 43.

3. Charles Mylander, *More Energy for Your Day: Tap into God's Power for Everyday Living* (Newberg, OR: Barclay Press, 2001), pp. 88-90.

4. Winston Churchill, quoted in *Great Quotes from Great Leaders,* comp. Peggy Anderson (Lombard, IL: Celebrating Excellence Publishing, 1990), p. 4.